REHOBOTH BEACH

MICHAEL MORGAN

REHOBOTH BEACH

A HISTORY OF SURF & SAND

THE
History
PRESS

Published by The History Press
Charleston, SC 29403
www.historypress.net

First published 2009
Second printing 2010
Third printing 2013

ISBN 9781540219701

Library of Congress Cataloging-in-Publication Data

Morgan, Michael, 1943-
Rehoboth Beach : a history of surf and sand / Michael Morgan.
p. cm.
Includes bibliographical references.
ISBN 9781540219701
1. Rehoboth Beach (Del.)--History. I. Title.
F174.R44M67 2009
975.1'7--dc22
2009004893

CONTENTS

CONTENTS

PREFACE

Most visitors to Rehoboth Beach, Delaware, enjoy the sun, sand, surf, boardwalk and other amusements that are found in many seaside resorts. Rehoboth, however, has a rich history that began with the Native Americans who spent their summers here and includes the religious leaders who established the resort, the boom years of the 1920s and the dark times of World War II. There is much to be found in this brief history of the town that was once regarded as the "Nation's Summer Capital."

This book would not have been possible without the assistance of the kind folks who toil in the libraries, archives and museums of Delaware. In particular, I would like to thank Randy L. Goss at the Delaware Public Archives and Iris Snyder at the University of Delaware for their efforts in obtaining some of the illustrations for this book. I would also like to thank Nancy Alexander, executive director of the Rehoboth Beach Museum, for her efforts in obtaining images from the museum's collection. I would also like to thank my son, Tom, for his unflagging efforts in obtaining vintage images, as well as for taking a number of photographs for this book.

In addition, I would like to thank Hannah Cassilly at The History Press for her untiring support in this project. I would like to thank Mike Mills, Terry Plowman, Bruce Pringle, Ashley Dawson, Laren Hughes-Hall and the other editors of the *Delaware Coast Press* and the *Wave* who have supported the "Delaware Diary" and the "Sussex Journal" for the past two decades. Writing two weekly columns has put me in touch with numerous readers who have shared their knowledge of Rehoboth Beach with me.

Finally, I would like to thank my wife, Madelyn, for constant editorial advice and support. She read every word in this book numerous times and spent countless hours correcting my spelling, punctuation and grammar. Without her help, this book would not have been possible. Whatever errors remain are mine.

Chapter 1

IN THE BEGINNING

FIRST VACATIONERS

Long before Europeans arrived on the Delaware coast, Native Americans vacationed at Rehoboth. Five centuries ago, scores of Native American communities were scattered about the Delmarva Peninsula. Between the high dunes of Cape Henlopen and the head of Rehoboth Bay, the mainland ran all the way to the surf. Several freshwater ponds punctuated this narrow stretch of woodland and beach. The bay and ponds provided oysters, fish and water. The ocean generated cool sea breezes, and during the hot summer months, the Native Americans left their permanent inland homes to vacation at the beach.

The Native Americans of Delmarva had no wheeled vehicles or horses, and they arrived at the beach on foot. About five hundred feet from the beach, there was a level area that ran parallel to the coast. Except for a low ridge of sand hills that divided the area in half, the level band of ground ran for about three quarters of a mile before it ended a little north of Rehoboth Bay. The Indians may have been Lenapes, who dominated the area north of Cape Henlopen, or they may have been Nanticokes, who lived between the coast and the river that bears their name. They set up bark huts that would serve as their homes during summer encampment on that strip of land that paralleled the beach.

Into the waters of Rehoboth Bay, the Native Americans would launch their dugout canoes. After a suitable tree had been felled and the branches removed, the Native Americans used shells to scrape off the tree trunk's bark to create a smooth log. Gum and resin were spread on top of the log and ignited. After the fire had charred the top of the log, the burned wood was scraped off. By alternately burning and scraping, the center area was hollowed out to create a solid wood canoe that was stable, sturdy and could be easily launched.

Native Americans camped near the head of Rehoboth Bay long before the Europeans arrived. *Diorama, Nanticoke Indian Museum, Millsboro, Delaware. Photo by Michael Morgan.*

After their huts were erected and their canoes ready for a day of fishing on Rehoboth Bay, the Native Americans settled down for a quiet vacation at the beach. With fish and oysters readily available in the nearby waters and game abounding in the surrounding forest, the Native Americans feasted on oysters, clams, crabs, turtles, fish and a variety of ducks, geese and other wildfowl. Cooked on open fires near their huts, the summer feasts led to an accumulation of shells, bones and other debris that the Native Americans swept into small conical mounds before they returned to their permanent homes in the interior of the Delmarva Peninsula.

The summer visits by the Native Americans went uninterrupted for many years. Out beyond the breaking surf, the ocean seemed endless; but one day, the white sails of vessels far larger than the familiar dugout canoes would be seen making their way along the horizon.

EXPLORERS ALONG THE COAST

The Native Americans at the head of Rehoboth Bay were probably enjoying their usual summer visit to the beach when Christopher Columbus began his epic voyage to America. After Columbus returned to Spain, the news of his discoveries spread across Europe, and scores of captains headed westward into the Atlantic in search of new lands. Most of these daring explorers were well aware of the dangers of sailing in uncharted waters, and it was not at all reassuring that on Christmas Day 1492 the *Santa Maria* struck a reef and sank off Hispaniola. Columbus returned to Europe on one of his other three ships, but a European explorer who sailed the North American coast in the sixteenth century was well advised to remain in deep waters. This was advice that Giovanni da Verrazzano was determined to heed.

Verrazzano was born in Florence in the late fifteenth century, when Italian captains had conquered the Mediterranean Sea and began to search for an all-water route to the Orient. When Christopher Columbus made his electrifying voyage in 1492, he was convinced that the islands of the West Indies lay near the coast of Asia. For decades following the first European contact with the New World, explorers continued to probe North, South and Central America in hopes of finding a water route to the lucrative markets of the Far East.

Verrazzano's parents were associated with the silk merchants of southern France. Buoyed by his family's fortune, he was educated in France, and he

A monument to the cautious Verrazzano stands at the foot of Olive Avenue. *Photo by Tom Morgan.*

11

developed into a capable navigator. In 1524, Verrazzano set sail aboard a small ship, *La Dauphine*, to continue the search for the elusive water route around America. When Verrazzano reached the coast of the Delmarva Peninsula, the explorer was determined that *La Dauphine* would not meet the same fate as the *Santa Maria*. As he sailed past the site of Rehoboth Beach, Verrazzano was so far from the coast that he failed to spot the entrance to Delaware Bay. His ship, however, would have been visible to any Native Americans on the beach near Rehoboth. After he continued northward, the cautious explorer entered the mouth of the Hudson River before he turned *La Dauphine* eastward and headed home.

Verrazzano's inability to find a water passage to the East cooled European interest in North America. It was not until 1609 that Henry Hudson became the first documented European to sail around Cape Henlopen and enter the bay. Verrazzano's voyage along the coast was a significant step in the exploration of North America. And when a monument to the explorer was recently dedicated at Olive Avenue and the boardwalk in Rehoboth Beach, he had finally made his way to the Delaware shore.

CAPTAIN AVERY BUILDS A HOME

Other mariners followed Henry Hudson's short foray into Delaware Bay, and by the middle of the seventeenth century, a small Dutch and Swedish settlement had been established at Lewes, just west of Cape Henlopen. In 1674, these Dutch and Swedish colonists who had settled near the mouth of the Delaware Bay were too occupied with clearing the land, producing enough food for the next winter and fending off attacks by pirates to be concerned with the repercussions of European politics. For many years, the small settlement on Lewes Creek was batted about in a game of political ping-pong as ownership of the south shore of Delaware Bay passed from Holland to Sweden, back to Holland and finally to England.

As part of the Treaty of Westminster that ended a war between England and Holland, the Dutch colonies in North America were transferred to English rule. Control of the Dutch settlements along the Hudson and Delaware Rivers passed to the Duke of York, brother of the king of England, and the duke appointed Edmund Andros as the governor of his new American possessions. Andros sought to clarify the southern boundary of the colony, and he took steps to protect the settlers against attacks by their Maryland neighbors. In 1673, three dozen armed Marylanders burned Lewes to the ground. Although the Duke of York and Lord Baltimore had agreed that the southern boundary of the Delaware colony was at Cape Henlopen, Andros began to enlarge the duke's holdings by giving English colonists grants of land on the shores of the Indian River and Rehoboth Bay. The English settlers established farms on the land granted to them by Andros in the name of the Duke of York, and their presence deterred the Marylanders from making direct attacks on the Delaware settlements. One such settler was Captain John Avery.

When Avery settled on the Delaware coast, he may have already decided that his seafaring days were over. Avery established a home on 350 acres of land on the north shore of Rehoboth Bay near King's Creek, west of the freshwater ponds that lined the coast. It was also near the area where Native Americans had often camped during the summer to fish and to enjoy the cool ocean breezes. The retired mariner dubbed his new home Avery's Rest. John Avery, however, had not abandoned all of his sailor's ways.

When the first European settlers arrived in Sussex County in the seventeenth century, the colonists built homes that were small, unrefined structures that barely protected the occupants from the elements. Avery and other coastal colonists felled trees with axes and saws and then cut logs into planks using broad axes and two-man pitsaws, where one stood on top of the log and the other beneath to give maximum power to each stroke of the saw. Wooden planks were used for the floors and roofs. Walls were often "wattle and daub," a process in which a series of woven wooden branches covered by clay gave the wall a finished appearance.

Some of the wooden houses built by the early settlers of Sussex County were tiny buildings that contained fewer than four hundred square feet. The first floor of these small homes contained one or two multipurpose rooms that were furnished with tables, chests, beds and other items. Chests served as seats as well as storage containers; tables served as counters where meals could be prepared and eaten. At night, furniture could be shifted and the floor became a common sleeping area.

When Avery built his home near the head of Rehoboth Bay, the Sussex County seat was at Lewes, where disputes between colonists were adjudicated. The existing court records illustrate the bickering that erupted among the settlers. Perhaps John Johnson Jr. was working too hard, or maybe he was bored, but in December 1680 he composed a song about Samuel Gray and his wife. According to court records:

The plaintiff declared that the defendant did sing a scurrilous disgraceful song of the plaintiff and his wife, for which the court fined him 500 pounds of tobacco or to be whipped 21 lashes on the naked back.

In April 1681, Avery was involved in a dispute with Andrew Evenne, and when the case was heard in the Lewes courtroom, Avery

> *broke in a great rage and fury, and called the court a company of rouges and pitiful fellows, and particularly, he called the president of the court "bastard" and said that the governor had as good sent his bald dog to have called him to an account…and said that he would make his sword walk tomorrow; and further, said he would pull them down a little lower before tomorrow night.*

The Lewes court was not about to take this abuse lightly, and a month later it gave Avery a chance to disavow his contemptuous remarks. The unrepentant Avery refused to recant what he had said. According to the court records:

> *The court offered that if the said Captain Avery would acknowledge his gross abuse of the king's court and crave them to pass it by promising to behave himself better…that they would pass it by; otherwise the court fine him for such abuse and contempt of the king's court as aforesaid the sum of ten pounds sterling money…to which the said Captain John Avery replied that he would see the devil take us all before he would.*

After this second outburst, the court ordered that Avery should be fined ten pounds sterling.

Despite swearing like the sailor that he was, Avery seems to have been forgiven by the growing community near Cape Henlopen. A short time later, the Duke of York turned over his holdings on the Delaware Bay to William Penn, who was very interested in substantiating his claim to land along the Atlantic coast. In a letter to Maryland officials, the Quaker leader's secretary pointed out:

> *In the year 1682, Wm. Penn…obtained a grant from the king's dearest brother James, Duke of York, for the counties of New Castle, Kent, Sussex, now so called, and in the said year, came over until this government and having gone down in person, and viewed the southernmost bound of… Sussex County.*

A year later, William Penn nominated John Avery, whom he addressed as one of his "Loving Friends," to be a justice of the peace for Sussex County. Avery, however, passed away a short time later, but the land between Rehoboth Bay and Cape Henlopen had been firmly established as part of Delaware.

In the Beginning

THE TREASURE OF CAPTAIN KIDD

Captain Kidd paid little heed as he sailed the *Saint Antonio* past the beach near the head of Rehoboth Bay, but the buccaneer watched carefully when he guided his vessel around the gentle curve of Cape Henlopen. After he dropped anchor near Cape Henlopen, Kidd welcomed several residents of Lewes aboard the *Saint Antonio*. The flabbergasted visitors reported that there were tons of treasure aboard the ship, and they bought some of the pirate loot.

The activities of the next few days were legendary. The townsfolk from Lewes landed some of the illicit cargo; the pirates transferred some of the ill-gotten goods to the sloop, and one of the sailors rowed to Cape Henlopen with a chest filled with his share of the treasure.

James Kelly was an everyday rogue of the sea who sometimes sailed under the names James Gilliam and Sampson Marshall. After several years of raiding defenseless vessels, Kelly landed at Madagascar, where he met Captain William Kidd. A New York colonist, Kidd had led an exemplary life until he was dispatched to the Indian Ocean, where he attempted to suppress the pirates who were raiding English ships. After Kidd captured several ships, he decided to turn pirate. With the *Saint Antonio* filled with loot, Kidd headed home to America. When he stopped at Madagascar, Kidd welcomed the veteran pirate Kelly aboard his ship.

In *The Book of Buried Treasure*, Ralph D. Paine described Kidd's voyage home:

> *Captain Kidd steered his sloop for the American coast and first touched at the fishing hamlet of Lewes at the mouth of Delware Bay. All legend to the contrary, he made no calls along the Carolinas and Virginia to bury treasure. The testimony of Kidd's crew and passengers cannot be demolished on this score... The first episode that smacks in the least of buried treasure occurred while the sloop was anchored off Lewes.*

What transpired while Kidd stopped at Lewes has been a puzzle that historians have been trying to solve for centuries. Writing in *Lippincott's Magazine* in 1882, William Barr Todd described Kidd's arrival at Lewes: "Off Cape Henlopen, he altered his course, sailed into Delware Bay, and put on shore a chest of treasure belonging to one James Gilliam, a passenger who had come on board at Madagascar."

As mentioned previously, James Gilliam was one of several aliases used by James Kelly, who failed to mention the stop at Lewes in his summary of his practical activities. After his capture, he refused to tell the authorities where

The grounds of Peter Marsh's Homestead became a landmark in Rehoboth. *Courtesy of the University of Delaware, Newark, Delaware.*

his loot was hidden. Initiated by stories from the Lewes townsfolk of the fabulous treasure aboard Kidd's ship and fueled by reports of pirates rowing to Cape Henlopen from the *Saint Antonio*, rumors of pirate loot hidden in the sands of the coast ran rampant among Delaware colonists.

Nearly half a century after Kidd's visit to Lewes, Peter Marsh acquired a tract of land south of Cape Henlopen that was near John Avery's old house, which had fallen into disrepair. While most Delaware colonists disdained living close to the beach, where the salt air was toxic to plants and the mosquitoes unsavory to humans, Marsh became one of the first colonists to live close to the surf. In 1743, he built a plantation home within walking distance of the beach. Marsh used durable brick, black walnut and cypress shingles to construct his two-story mansion, which was dubbed the Homestead.

Legend has it that Marsh lived close to the dunes so that he could search for the lost treasure of Captain Kidd. As far as is known, he never uncovered a single doubloon of pirate gold from either Kidd or the petty pirate James Kelly. Marsh's sturdily constructed colonial home, however, remained a fixture of the Rehoboth landscape for centuries to come.

CHAPTER 2

A NEW RESORT IS BORN

MORE VACATIONERS ARRIVE

"To bathe in the sea," John Floyer commented in the early eighteenth century, "is to have not only a cold bath, but a medicinal cold bath." Although Floyer offered his advice when European colonists were moving into the Rehoboth area, they saw little benefit in taking a dip in the ocean. At that time, many people believed that diseases germinated in water, and to plunge into any water, especially the cold surf of the Atlantic Ocean, seemed to invite disaster.

When Floyer published *The History of Cold Bathing* in 1702, he noted that parents believed it was immodest to bathe their children: "Parents…could not justify these prejudices, without crying down cold baths as dangerous. And since they now further object, that it never was the custom to immerse children in England."

For Floyer, the lack of interest in a dip in the ocean could be traced to the rise of England as a global economic power:

> *I shall add one more reason of the disuse of cold baths, which was the increase and interest of foreign trade in the last century, which then introduc'd all the hot regimen from the hot climates, such as tobacco, tea, coffee, wine, and brandy spirits, and spices, and these are unnatural to English bodies; for a cold regimen is proper to cold countries, as the hot regimen for hot regions, because they preserve our bodies in a state suitable to the ambient air. If we stop the pores by a cold regimen in hot countries, a fever and fluxes immediately succeed; and if we keep them open by a hot regimen in cold countries, defluxions and intermittent fevers, and faintness happen.*

Floyer's *History of Cold Bathing* failed to send people scurrying to the beach for a dip in the surf, but it helped alleviate some of their fear of water. While it would take many years for most folks' attitudes toward a frolic in the surf to change, some people found another reason to visit Rehoboth: oysters.

In 1790, the proprietor of the Oyster House in Frederica, Delaware, announced that at his establishment "gentlemen and ladies will meet with good entertainment," and to ensure that his customers feasted on the highest quality oysters, the owner of the new inn proclaimed that "he has engaged Oysters from Rehoboth Bay once a month, until they are out of season."

In the nineteenth century, oysters continued to be standard fare on many dinner tables, and as the Native Americans had discovered, some of the best oysters came from Rehoboth Bay. A century and a half ago, cooks never tired of developing new ways to serve the bivalve. When the noted English writer Charles Mackay visited America, he discovered

oysters pickled, stewed, baked, roasted, fried, and scalloped; oysters made into soups, patties, and puddings; oysters with condiments and without condiments; oysters for breakfast, dinner, and supper; oysters without sting or limit, fresh as the fresh air, and almost as abundant.

By 1852, the industrious watermen had depleted many of the oyster beds, and the Delaware state legislature prohibited oystering from May 1 through August 10. During these months, Delaware diners longed for a taste of the local bivalves, and by the beginning of August, devotees of oysters impatiently waited to taste their favorite food again. During the first year that the restrictions went into effect, August 10 fell on the second Thursday of the month, and on that day, the crews and their families celebrated the opening of the dredging season. The day quickly became an annual event that was dubbed "Big Thursday," which developed into a major summer celebration. Families from southern Delaware gathered at oyster landings so that they would be on hand when the first boats arrived. While some oysters were being fried, stewed, scalloped and prepared in a variety of other dishes, others were shucked and immediately eaten raw. While the cooks prepared the bivalves, the crowd sang, danced and enjoyed other amusements.

Although oysters may have given Rehoboth Bay its first taste of renown, they failed to attract visitors to the beach. By the middle of the nineteenth century, the attitudes of Sussex County residents toward the beach began to change, and they began to look away from Rehoboth Bay, where they had been harvesting oysters, to the beach, where the surf offered an opportunity for a cool ocean bath.

In 1855, Robert West purchased a tract of land near the head of Rehoboth Bay, where he proposed building a "summer retreat and bathing place" that

A New Resort Is Born

Many early visitors to the beach enjoyed the cooling pines and sea breezes. *Courtesy of the Rehoboth Beach Historical Society.*

was named Rehoboth Beach. Although West was able to attract several investors to his beachfront project, it failed to get off the ground. When the Civil War began five years later, interest in an ocean resort at Rehoboth was put on hold. But West's attempt to establish a resort south of Cape Henlopen would one day bear fruit.

THE SEA HATH SPOKEN

Shortly after the end of the Civil War, Reverend Robert W. Todd, the pastor of St. Paul's Methodist Episcopal Church in Wilmington, had been exhausted by several weeks of strenuous work when he decided to visit Ocean Grove on the New Jersey coast for a little rest and relaxation. After his refreshing visit to the beach, Todd returned to Wilmington to share an account of his exhilarating experience with his congregation in a sermon entitled "And the Sea Hath Spoken." Reverend Todd was so enthusiastic about the benefits of a visit to the seacoast that he decided to establish a summer retreat near Ocean Grove for his congregation. When he discovered that the price of land in New Jersey was prohibitively high, Todd turned his attention to the Delmarva Peninsula. As he searched for a suitable location, he mused, "Why, cannot we have a Christian seashore for this Peninsula and the regions adjoining and beyond?"

Some years earlier, Todd had heard of Richard West's abortive attempt to establish a "summer retreat and bathing place" just north of Rehoboth Bay. Here, quiet pine woods, freshwater ponds, a bay brimming with oysters, a wide pristine beach and the rolling ocean surf were within steps of one another. Todd had found the place for his seaside retreat. After a committee of ministers and laymen visited the spot between the head of Rehoboth Bay and the sands of Cape Henlopen, they pronounced it ideal for a seaside resort and recommended that it be purchased immediately.

The Rehoboth Beach Camp Meeting Association of the Methodist Episcopal Church was formed to buy the land, lay the streets and sell the lots. At Rehoboth, the mainland ran down to the surf, and the Camp Meeting Association laid out a town that was shaped somewhat like a triangle, with its base at the beach and its two longer sides extending inland. The town's principal streets radiated from the camp grove located at the inland point of the triangle toward the beach. A wide street ran along the base of the triangle near the dunes. To make it easy to move about the resort, the association planned to have a line of horsecars that would run from the camp grove down Rehoboth Avenue to the beach, where it would turn north along Surf Avenue. At Park Avenue, the horsecars would turn inland and run back to the campgrounds. This arrangement meant that there were few lots that faced the ocean. The early vacationers at Rehoboth were interested in enjoying the regenerative effect of the cool sea breezes and the soothing sounds of the waves, as well as attending church services.

In July 1873, the association published the *Rehoboth Beacon*, which pointed out that the building lots and streets

> *as shown on the plat are laid out with a view of plenty of room, air and sunshine, and exemption from ravages of the fire fiend; and also to secure the least possible obstruction to the view from various localities and cottages.*

The *Beacon* also provided a progress report on the new Delaware resort:

> *The amount of grading done principally on Surf and Rehoboth Avenues, both very broad, is estimated to be equal to the grading of about ten miles of railroad in the Peninsula. Besides which the grounds have been entirely laid out, and to a large extent enclosed with substantial fencing. During the warm season, the work of grading will be suspended but will be resumed in the fall and spring at various points, thus opening the grounds and preparing the way for vigorous cottage building during the spring and summer of 1874.*

A New Resort Is Born

The new resort's main street was Rehoboth Avenue, which ran from the camp grove to the beach. According to the *Rehoboth Beacon*, this grand thoroughfare

> *is three-fourths of a mile in length, one hundred feet wide at the grove, two feet at the sea. It is designed to be one of the grandest avenues in the world, when built up and shaded with handsome trees as we think it may be in a few years. It affords a fine view of the ocean. Paved sidewalks and other improvements will come in due time.*

Surf Avenue, the resort's second most important street, was

> *100 feet wide* [and] *extends along the bluffs parallel with the ocean shore. It is neatly graded to a point north of the Hotel, and will make a good drive, with the breakers rolling near by in full view. At low tide a fine drive is afford by the sand-paved margin of the sea, for several miles in the direction of Cape Henlopen; the sand having become so packed by the action of the water as scarcely to show a horse's footprints.*

Although the lots sold quickly, weather delayed the construction of many buildings. According to the *Rehoboth Beacon*, cottage building

> *has been delayed and interfered with by the backwardness of the season, and consequent delay of the work of the association; but we are looking for the erection of a large number of cottages in time for the second season.*

The poor weather may have delayed the construction of cottages, but other facilities were being built at a quick pace. The *Beacon* reported:

> *The arrangements for boarding are as extensive and complete as could be well secured in the limited time during which we have to work. The large and comfortable hotel containing on the second and third floors thirty-eight good sleeping rooms, and an attic on the fourth floor that could be used in an emergency, will be under the management of Mrs. Mary H. Keene of Wilmington, Delaware whose reputation is a sufficient guarantee of comfort to the boarders.*

In addition, several people who had completed their cottages made arrangements to take in boarders during the summer season.

THE DELAWARE SUMMER RESORT

REHOBOTH BEACH

ON THE ATLANTIC OCEAN NEAR CAPE HENLOPEN, OPPOSITE CAPE MAY

"WHERE PINE WOODS AND OCEAN WAVES MEET"

Built on solid land in the prosperous and garden county of Sussex. In the center of the peach and small fruit belt.

Surrounded by truck farms

Abundance of

sea food

Living expenses

less.

No stagnant marshes

No malaria

Electric lights

Gas

EXCELLENT WATER

Sailing and fishing on Rehoboth Bay

Surrounded by pine woods

Safest and best ocean

bathing in America

W. A. HORN

Real Estate

and

Cottages

for sale or

rent

BUILDING LOTS CHEAP

ATLANTIC OCEAN

REHOBOTH BEACH

The nearest ocean resort to Baltimore and Washington

YOUR OPPORTUNITY

The streets of Rehoboth were laid out quickly, and real estate developers sprang into action. *Courtesy of Marcella Dawson.*

Finally, construction was underway on

> *a two story plank tent on the camp ground 20 x 64 feet which will afford comfortable entertainment to a large number of persons during the summer season; and Miss Jennie Montgomery of Felton, and E.J. Morris, Esq., Lewes, Delware will each conduct a boarding tent during the camp meeting. We think that there will be enough to eat, and several baskets of fragments left over.*

Reverend Todd had been discouraged by the high cost of lots on the New Jersey shore, and the lots in Rehoboth were more reasonably priced:

> *There are about one thousand lots unsold, ranging from $75 to $150, many of them very desirable. The northern portion of our grounds, now nearly covered over with the growth of young pine and cedar timber, remains to be developed and is destined to become very popular, when the designs of the plat shall be executed.*

It did not take long for many of the empty lots to be filled in with buildings, and Reverend Robert Todd's vision of a seaside resort on the shores of the Delaware coast soon became a reality. The sea had spoken.

A New Resort Is Born

CAMP MEETING IN THE PINES

A century before the Rehoboth Beach Camp Meeting Association was formed by the Methodist Episcopal Church, followers of John and Charles Wesley, George Whitefield and other Methodists were prohibited from speaking in many established churches. These eloquent itinerant preachers spoke in barns, fields and other places where large numbers of people gathered to hear them. Writing in 1859, the Methodist historian John Lendum described how the young preacher Freeborn Garrettson was received by the people of southern Delaware:

> *The 1ˢᵗ of April, 1779, Mr. Garrettson was led by Divine Providence into the region of the Cypress Swamp, in Sussex County, Delaware, to a place called the Sound. After preaching five or six sermons, that were a hammer and a fire, to break and melt the hearts of the people, he read and explained the rules of the Methodists; and examined and admitted about forty weeping penitents into a society, which has continued ever since. The*

Visitors to the camp meetings stayed in small wooden cottages know as "tents." *Photo by Tom Morgan.*

23

people were so much interested in having him preach, that they came ten and twelve miles on foot.

Lendum went on to point out that the lack of established churches in parts of southern Delaware helped make the residents of Sussex County receptive to itinerant Methodist preachers, and they began to hold camp meetings where people gathered for several days to listen to the preachers, read the Bible and contemplate the state of their religion. In his autobiography, William Morgan (a Sussex County doctor and Methodist preacher) described the tent that he used at an early camp meeting:

I, yes I, had the large tent. It was made on this wise, two sheets were sewed together at one end with loops tacked to the other ends. Two crutches were set in the ground about five feet high, a pole laid on them as the sheets were wide. The sheets were thrown over and pinned to the ground with wooden sticks driven through the loops.

While attending this camp meeting, Morgan slept on a mattress of leaves that was covered by a blanket. Although the beds may have been primitive, the food was more than adequate. According to Morgan:

A pone of bread and biscuits with a boiled ham or chicken or cheese were taken out in a bag or trunk or gig box, a knife, a tin cup or mug, served instead of cups and saucers. All sat on the ground or stood up to eat, taking it in their hands they eat their meals with the singleness of heart and praised God. Few eat or drank to gluttony, and no ado about a fine show of tents or victuals, or trouble to wash dishes and the like.

By the middle of the nineteenth century, the camp meetings had become a permanent fixture in southern Delaware. When Reverend Todd and the Rehoboth Beach Camp Meeting Association established their seaside retreat, the meeting grounds were placed at the west end of town. In a grove shaded by tall pine trees, the Rehoboth meeting grounds featured a rectangular pulpit for the preacher and rows of seats for the congregation. Instead of the tents described by Morgan, simple frame houses, known as "tents," had sprung up on the resort's streets. Most of these buildings were three-hundred-square-foot wooden structures divided into two rooms with no heat, electricity or indoor plumbing.

The wooden "tents" were adequate for the early visitors to Rehoboth Beach. Within a few years, however, other vacationers began to arrive at Rehoboth, and these folks were interested in more elaborate accommodations. They began to erect more lavish summer cottages. It was not long before a few year-round homes were sprinkled among the camp meeting tents and cottages.

As Rehoboth Beach developed into a permanent seaside community, it attracted visitors and residents who had no interest in the activities of the camp meeting. Soon, some of the ministers who preached at the meeting grounds began to lament the decline in morals at Rehoboth. One railed against dancing as one of the "lowest and most vulgar amusements." Another preacher declared that Rehoboth had become "a den of dancing, card playing and whiskey drinking." Although the Camp Meeting Association endeavored to maintain the religious nature of the resort, in 1879 it changed its name to the Rehoboth Beach Association. Two years later, the camp meetings were discontinued by their founding organization.

THE RAILROAD CHUGS INTO TOWN

"The Frenchtown and New Castle Railroad," a Baltimore newspaper announced in 1832, long before Reverend Todd was inspired to establish a seaside camp meeting,

> *was opened for transportation of persons and goods on Thursday last. It may and will be very rapidly traveled by steam-power because of its extraordinary straightness. One of the coaches built to run upon it by the famous Imlay of Baltimore, may well be called a traveling "palace," because of its conveniences, and it will comfortably seat fifty persons inside and out.*

At a time when the speed of all other land travel was determined by the pace of an animal, the speed of a train seemed to test the limits that a person could endure. When the Frenchtown and New Castle Railroad began operating, the engineers were ordered to limit the speed of the trains to twelve miles per hour, but by the time that the railroad reached the coast, trains could easily travel more than forty miles per hour.

Early train travel may have been exhilarating, but it was not without its hazards. During an age when people dressed up to travel, the soot and cinders that spewed from the engine's smokestack invaded the passenger cars and showered the passengers. According to historian John C. Hayman:

The railroad revolutionized travel to Rehoboth. *Courtesy of the Rehoboth Beach Historical Society.*

The wooden seats in the old coaches were hard and the clouds of smoke and cinders from the engine were annoying. A routine task at the end of such a trip for a mother was to beat the soot from her children's clothes.

A century ago, when kids across Delmarva heard the whistle of an approaching train, they rushed to a vantage point near the tracks to watch as the train raced by. Years later, one Eastern Shore youth who eagerly watched a train fly past on the way to the beach later commented, "The train was the embodiment of all that was romantic and exciting."

Four years after the opening of the Frenchtown and New Castle Railroad, plans were made to run track southward down the length of Delaware, but economic conditions and the Civil War delayed the construction for decades. In 1878, five years after the resort was established, the first train came chugging into Rehoboth. Initially, the tracks stopped at the camp meeting grounds, but six yeas later, the line was extended down Rehoboth Avenue to a new depot near the center of town.

The opening of the train line to the resort provided vacationers from Washington, Baltimore and other cities easy access to Rehoboth Beach. In an era when the most luxurious form of land transportation meant traveling along dusty, unpaved roads behind a team of animals whose barnyard aroma did little to enhance the ambiance of the experience, a railroad coach was a

The train carried vacationers into the center of town. *Courtesy of the Rehoboth Beach Historical Society.*

6:—THE CAR AMONGST THE PINES, REHOBOTH BEACH, DEL.

Some train cars came to town and stayed for decades. *Courtesy of the University of Delaware, Newark, Delaware.*

rolling palace. In addition, some trains pulled private cars that were outfitted with a stateroom with a full double bed, a dining room with a full-size table and chairs and a bathroom. A private car was parked among the trees in Rehoboth, where it was used as a vacation home for over half a century.

For several decades, the train station near the end of Rehoboth Avenue was a hub of activity as passengers disembarked within sight of the pounding surf. For the next generation, railroads would dominate transportation until they were displaced by the automobile in the early twentieth century.

THE EARLY PLEASURES OF THE BEACH

With the railroad providing easy access to the beach, the popularity of vacationing at Rehoboth began to spread to residents of cities all along the East Coast. In June 1885, the *New York Times* advised its readers that "a host of pleasure resorts [are] within easy reach of the city with attractions to suit all classes and all purses." After describing the mountain and ocean resorts that were close to New York, the newspaper pointed out that "a sea trip, robbed of its dangers can also be pleasantly made to Norfolk, Old Point Comfort, Newport News, and Rehoboth Beach."

When the vacationers disembarked from the train, they headed to newly erected rooming houses and hotels. The Surf House, which was constructed in 1873, when Rehoboth was established, was destroyed by fire in 1879, but the Henlopen Hotel, with about seventy-five rooms, was erected nearby. In addition, Rehoboth boasted a recently refurbished hotel operated by William Bright, a Wilmington industrialist. During the Civil War, Bright's Southern leanings led to his arrest and an extended stay in Fort Delaware. Bright's imprisonment broke his health, and after the war he moved to Rehoboth, where he made the eighty-room Bright House one of the resort's premier establishments.

Excellent accommodations were also provided by the Douglass House, a sixty-room hotel located a short distance south of Rehoboth. Historian J. Thomas Scharf noted that there were in Rehoboth "several large boarding houses and there were about forty cottages. Ten of the latter were occupied the entire year." According to Scharf, "Among the improvements here projected is an iron pier into the ocean, to enable steamers of light draft to effect a landing." Although a pier was eventually constructed, it was used for fishing and not as a landing for steamboats.

As Rehoboth grew, visitors learned to take a dip in the surf. Swimming was still a novelty, but many people were following Floyer's advice to venture

A New Resort Is Born

The Henlopen Hotel was one of Rehoboth's enduring landmarks. *Courtesy of the University of Delaware, Newark, Delaware.*

into the surf and take an "Ocean Bath." When the resort was established, the *Rehoboth Beacon* noted that the bathing at the Delaware resort

> *cannot be excelled. All the shore is a broad, level plateau, extending for more than one hundred yards from the margin of the water; and affording a bathing ground which at half tide or low water is perfectly safe for any person of ordinary prudence.*

At that time, there were no lifeguards on the beach, but "the usual precautions will be employed to guard against accident during the season, and ample means taken to afford comfortable and convenient facilities for bathing."

In 1890, Duffield Osborne described the dramatic growth of ocean beaches in *Scribner's Magazine*. As Rehoboth grew, many vacationers were learning how to deal with the pounding surf, and Osborne's article "Surf and Surf Bathing" provided much-needed advice:

> *There are few, nowadays, who do not appreciate the privilege of playing with the Atlantic Ocean; but perhaps there are fewer still who have ever taken the trouble to study the character and humors of their playmate—for he is full of tricks, this same ocean, and his jests are sometimes sadly practical; he is all life and good spirits—the jolliest of joy company—when*

29

By the end of the nineteenth century, vacationers were learning to frolic in the ocean. *Courtesy of the Rehoboth Beach Historical Society.*

he is in the humor; but he must be treated with tact, tact born of knowledge of his ways and moods; and above all, his would-be friends must learn to recognize when he is really angry, and then they must leave him to rave or grumble alone until boisterous good-nature resumes its sway.

Osborne provided tips on judging the size of an ocean wave, and he gave specific instructions on how to dive into the surf without being tossed head over heels:

Dive just as you would from a low shore, only not quite so much downward—say at an angle of twenty degrees off the horizontal; your object being to slip under the incoming volume of water, to get somewhat into the "under-tow," and yet to run no risk of running afoul of the bottom. The heavier the wave, the deeper will be the water in which you can stand, and the deeper you can and should dive.

Osborne also described how a gentleman should help a lady enter the surf. He advised the couple to stand facing each other. As they awaited the next wave, Osborne instructed the man to place his hands on his companion's waist:

A New Resort Is Born

You thus stand with your left and her right side toward the ocean, and as the wave rises before you, your companion should, at the word, spring from the sand while at the same moment you swing her around with all your force, and throw her backward into the advancing breaker.

For those who objected that flinging a person into a breaking wave may not be the best way for them to enjoy the surf, Osborne suggested a second method: "Let her stand directly in front of and facing you. Standing thus, she springs and is pushed backward through the wave somewhat as in the former instance."

Although it is impossible to know how many vacationers on the Delaware coast followed Osborne's advice, a booster of Rehoboth Beach echoed his feelings on the irresistibility of the surf:

The bathing at Rehoboth Beach is about as good as there is on the Atlantic Coast. Here the briny surf invites one as enticingly as it does elsewhere… The sea rarely if ever kisses a better beach than Rehoboth Beach. It has been so many years since the site of the present town was used for a camp-meeting, but there has been a great transformation in the intervening years. Where only a somber pine thicket, with an intervening waste of sea grass and sand dunes, once bordered the ocean, now there has risen a splendid town to cheer, with its glare of lights, the lonely coast.

Many vacationers enjoyed a day at the beach without getting wet. *Courtesy of the University of Delaware, Newark, Delaware.*

31

THE SURFMEN PROTECT THE BEACH

"It was a drama in one short act," Frances A. Doughty wrote in 1893,

> *played to an orchestral accompaniment from the neighboring Plaza or the more distant Midway, the sun beaming joyously down on the man who was pretending to be wrecked, while shouts of laughter and applause attended to his jumping into the "breeches-buoy" and his safe convoy, with dangling legs, across the sparkling waters.*

When the World's Columbian Exposition was held in Chicago in 1893 to commemorate the 400th anniversary of the voyage of Christopher Columbus to America, more than twenty-seven million people visited the collection of faux marble buildings, affectionately called the "White City." Following the Civil War, the Life-Saving Service, which had been established to assist sailors in distress, and its precision demonstration by six surfmen armed with a small cannon, ropes and a rowboat,

The Rehoboth Beach Life-Saving Station stood south of town. *Courtesy of the Delaware Public Archives.*

A New Resort Is Born

*was always a popular exhibition at the White City during that summer of
'93 which so many American citizens now recall as the most memorable
conjunction of pleasure with education they ever managed to effect.*

Residents of the Delaware coast who visited the Columbian Exposition
would have been very familiar with the drill. In 1878, the Rehoboth Beach Life-
Saving Station was built to plans by J. Lake Patterson and established just south
of the budding resort opposite the north end of Rehoboth Bay. All U.S. Life-
Saving stations followed a general plan that was similar to that of a modern fire
station. On the first floor, a large room contained the surfboat, which sat on a
light carriage with large wheels. At all times, the surfboat was ready to be rolled
across the beach and launched into the pounding waves. Also stored in the boat
room was a mortar cart that carried a Lyle gun and several hundred feet of
carefully arranged line. The Lyle gun was a small cannon that was used to fire
a line to a stranded ship. The first floor of each station also contained a kitchen
and an eating area for the surfmen. The second floor of the lifesaving station
was divided into two sleeping rooms and a storage area. Atop the station was a
lookout platform that gave the surfmen a good view of the ocean and beach.

Every Tuesday and Thursday, Keeper Thomas Truxton led the surfmen
of the Rehoboth Beach station through the drills that thrilled the crowds
at the Columbian Exposition. When the surfmen rolled the lifesaving
equipment onto the beach to practice with the Lyle gun, breeches buoy and
other equipment, vacationers gathered to watch. In 1897, Thomas W. Steele
succeeded Truxton as keeper, but the drills remained a hit with visitors.
According to an early promoter of the resort:

> *Rehoboth Beach Life Saving Station—A visit to this station is always a
> pleasant trip, and as it is only one mile distant, it makes a delightful surf
> walk. The Captain, T.W. Steele, is endowed with unlimited patience and
> good humor and takes pleasure in explaining the different appliances for
> saving life in case of a wreck.*

Echoing "the most memorable conjunction of pleasure with education"
experience at the Columbian Exposition, the drill at Rehoboth Beach was
proclaimed to be "both instructive and entertaining."

On those weekdays when public drills were not conducted, the surfmen
worked with the lifeboat, lines, blocks and other equipment. In addition,
they attended lessons on the international signal code and drilled on the
resuscitation of drowned persons. Saturday was devoted to housecleaning
chores, and Sunday was a day of rest.

According to Doughty:

> *Every rule and every regulation of the service is calculated to develop many virtues and to repress vices; for constant, hourly fidelity to duty cannot fail to operate favorably on character. To a great extent, however, character must have been already formed before a man can become a "Knight of the surf."*

The surfman's day did not end at sundown. The time from sundown to dawn was divided into three watches, and two surfmen were assigned to each watch to patrol the beach. At the start of each watch, two crewmen left from the station. One walked north until he met the surfman from the Cape Henlopen station; the other walked south until he encountered the surfman from the Indian River Inlet station. After a brief exchange of news and pleasantries, the men also exchanged tokens shaped like small badges to indicate that they had made contact. The men then retraced their steps to their home stations.

As they trudged along the beach, the surfmen carefully surveyed the ocean for a sign of a vessel in difficulty. Each man carried a Coston flare that was activated by a plunger that struck a charge, which, in turn, ignited brightly burning chemicals that produced a light that could be seen for many miles. Coston flares were simple to use, easy to carry and worked well in all types of weather.

According to Doughty:

> *A patrolman always carries, slung across his shoulder, a small satchel containing four Coston lights. If he has been signaled, and has answered according to the international code, his next duty is to return to his station as quickly as possible and report the occurrence, so that the crew can go to the aid of the ship in distress.*

When a surfman spotted a vessel venturing too close to shore or a ship in distress, he ignited his flare and held it high over his head as a sign to those aboard the ship that help was on the way. In addition, it was hoped that the bright light of the flare would alert other members of the lifesaving crew that a vessel was in distress, and preparations for a rescue could begin.

In an article published by *Harper's Magazine* in 1880, James Merryman described members of the Life-Saving Service on patrol:

A New Resort Is Born

The surfmen of the Rehoboth Beach Life-Saving Station were constantly on guard. *Courtesy of the University of Delaware, Newark, Delaware.*

> *The beach guardians are no idle promenaders. A march of four or five miles through the soft sea-sand is a task at any time; what is it in the fury of a winter storm? The prevalent strong winds, which must be encountered in one direction or the other of the beat, drive before them rain, snow, hail, and sleet, or oftener sharp sand, which cuts the face until, smarting with pain, the patrolman turns and walks backward for relief. Such is the forces of this natural sand-blast that it soon dulls the glass of the patrol lanterns, and some of the more exposed stations has made ground-glass of the window panes.*

For their efforts, the surfmen were paid sixty dollars a month. Surfmen paid for their own uniforms, which averaged thirty-five dollars a set. In addition, surfmen paid eight dollars a month for food and shared the cost of a cook. Although the pay may have been low and the conditions difficult, the surfmen were dedicated to their duties. According to legend, after a particularly difficult rescue that lasted many hours, the crew of surfmen finally reached shore. The keeper turned to his men and cheerfully announced, "Now boys, straighten up the house and let's get out a patrol!"

SOS OFF THE COAST

With the bone-numbing wind and the skin-crackling cold, no one wanted to be on the dunes the night of March 11, 1888, but a massive storm was battering dozens of vessels behind the Delaware Breakwater. The disaster was so great that crews from Lewes, Cape Henlopen, Rehoboth and Indian River Inlet were summoned to help save those on the ships in distress. Without hesitation, Keeper Thomas Truxton led the surfmen from the Rehoboth Beach Life-Saving Station across the sand.

When the surfmen reached the beach opposite the Breakwater, they could see several vessels in danger, but there was little they could do. Their brightly shining Colson flare was a small comfort to the frozen sailors who clung to the rigging of vessels whose hulls had begun to settle to the bottom. The surfmen attempted to string lines from the shore to the foundering ships, but they were frustrated by the howling winds and driving snow. Unable to reach the stranded sailors, the surfmen retreated to the lifesaving station until morning.

When March 12 dawned, the blizzard began to moderate, and the crews of the lifesaving stations returned to the beach, where they were confronted by more than twenty shipwrecks. Despite the heavy waves, a surfboat was launched, and after a Herculean effort, the small boat reached some of the damaged ships. Several sailors had already died from exposure, but nearly two hundred crewmen from the wrecked vessels were saved.

The great scale of the disaster in March 1888 had required the combined efforts of surfmen from four of the Delaware lifesaving stations. Such cooperation was not unusual. In November 1888, crews of the Rehoboth Beach and Cape Henlopen stations spotted the schooner *Ella*, from Bangor, Maine, having difficulty off the coast. The schooner was commanded by Captain W.D. Gates, who was bound for Philadelphia with a cargo of lumber. On November 25, the sailing vessel attempted to enter Delaware Bay during a heavy northeast gale. About noon, the strong winds blew the *Ella* southward past Cape Henlopen, and Gates decided to anchor until the winds subsided.

Surfmen from both lifesaving stations had been watching the struggling schooner for some time, and thinking that the captain of the *Ella* intended to beach it, they began to prepare for a rescue. When the schooner anchored, the surfmen put their rescue operation on hold, but they continued to keep a careful eye on the *Ella*. After two hours in the battering storm, the *Ella* began to leak badly, and Gates decided to slip the anchor cables and make a run for the beach. According to the annual report of the Life-Saving Service:

The life-savers were in readiness. After consultation by telephone it was decided what portions of the gear should be taken from each station, and the two crews set out. The vessel struck about one hundred yards from shore, a

A New Resort Is Born

mile and three quarters north of the Rehoboth Beach Station and three and half miles south of the Cape Henlopen Station.

Crews from both stations set out to assist the stranded schooner. The surfmen of the Rehoboth Beach station had a shorter distance to travel, but they were heading directly into the wind as they made their way across the beach. Led by Keeper Truxton, the surfmen transported the light gear in a wagon and used a team of horses to draw the heavy apparatus cart. According to the annual report:

The beach was badly cut through in many places by the surf, the gale constantly drove the cutting sand in their faces, and progress was necessarily slow, so that, although the other crew had a much greater distance to cover, all arrived at about the same time.

By the time the surfmen reached a position on the beach opposite the stranded schooner, the *Ella* had been blown broadside to the beach, and massive waves, some that were half-mast high, were breaking over the vessel. To avoid being swept into the sea, Gates and the crew of the *Ella* had climbed into the schooner's rigging. As the surfmen worked, they were assisted by a number of persons from Rehoboth who had gathered on the beach. The first firing of the Lyle gun threw a line across the vessel and landed it within reach of the stranded sailors. According to the annual report:

Huddled together, as the latter were, in awkward positions, drenched by the dashing spray, and cold from exposure, but obliged to cling desperately to avoid being swept into the riotous surf, they hauled off the whip line slowly and with extreme difficulty.

Although the work was slow and difficult, the lines for the breeches buoy were set up and the sailors were ferried ashore. The shipwrecked sailors were taken to the Rehoboth Beach station, where they stayed for a few days to recover from their ordeal. Several weeks later, Captain Gates wrote a letter of appreciation to the general superintendent of the Life-Saving Service:

Bangor, Maine, January 24, 1889

Dear Sir: I wish to express to the Life Saving Service my thanks and appreciation of the services rendered me and my crew on the 25th of November last…I shall ever keep in grateful remembrance the crew of

Rehoboth Beach Life-Saving Station, and Captain Truxton in particular, for his valuable assistance to me in the discharge of my duties about the wreck.

Very respectfully,
W.D. Gates
Master of the Schooner Ella

SURFMEN SAVE THE TOWN

The surfmen of the Rehoboth Beach Life-Saving Station provided a degree of protection for the mariners who sailed along the Delaware coast. In addition, these men helped meet some of the other needs of Rehoboth. In *The U.S. Life-Saving Service: Heroes, Rescues and Architecture of the Early Coast Guard,* Ralph Shanks and Wick York summarized the myriad chores performed by the surfmen:

Besides shipwrecks, the Life-Saving service frequently acted as physicians and nurses, policemen of the sea, fire fighters, life guards and more. They

A cry for help brought a throng of rescuers. *Courtesy of the University of Delaware, Newark, Delaware.*

38

A New Resort Is Born

thwarted suicides, aided imperiled swimmers, sheltered the homeless and the lost. They captured runaway boys, outlaws, teams of horses and lost pets. They recovered lost horses, bicycles, buoys, loads of hay, cows, pigs, sacks of mail, fish nets and eventually even automobiles. The Life-Saving Service was perhaps best described by the Coast Guard motto, Semper Paratus, *"Always ready."*

The keeper and surfmen of the Rehoboth station were recruited from the coastal area, and they were familiar with the peculiarities of the Delaware coast. James H. Merryman, chief inspector of the Life-Saving Service, wrote of the crews who manned the lifesaving stations:

Both keeper and men are chosen from among the fishermen in the vicinity of the stations, who are most distinguished for their ability as surfmen. Drawing their first breath within sound of the surf, they pass through childhood viewing the sea in all its moods…This life gives them familiarity with the portion of the beach upon which they dwell, and its bordering currents, eddies and bars, and an intimate acquaintance with the habits of the surf.

During the summer months, when the ocean was calmer and the chances of a shipwreck diminished, the surfmen were off duty, and Keeper Truxton was allowed to be away from the station for up to a week at a time. In July 1888, he was in the Bright House, where a number of vacationers were staying. Rehoboth was only fifteen years old, and many visitors to the young resort were still discovering the pleasures and dangers of the surf.

On July 23, Mrs. H.M. Schooley and Mr. W.M.S. Brown decided to go for an ocean bath in the surf. While the two bathers were enjoying their dip in the waves, they drifted slowly into deeper water. When the couple realized that they could not touch bottom, Schooley, who could not swim, panicked. Brown, who was a good swimmer, grabbed hold of Schooley and attempted to pull her toward shallow water. As the two struggled in the waves, they feared that they were on the verge of going under, and they screamed for help.

At that time, Rehoboth had no beach patrol or other organized lifesaving system, but the cries of the two drowning swimmers were heard by a teenager, C. Allen Maull of Lewes. Maull dashed into the waves and swam to the couple. He grabbed Schooley, who had hold of Brown. Maull was able to keep the two afloat, but he was not able to make any progress toward shore. All three were now in danger of drowning.

39

At the Bright House, Walter Burton, the manager of the hotel, and Keeper Truxton heard the cries and ran for the beach. Throwing off their coats and shoes, the two men dived into the surf. Burton reached Schooley and Maull and was able to bring them to the beach, but the ocean currents took Brown, who continued to scream for help, farther out to sea. According to the official report of the Life-Saving Service, "Keeper Thomas J. Truxton…sprang into the surf and by strong strokes soon reached the drowning man and brought him also in safety to the beach amid the plaudits of the assembled crowd." For their actions, both Maull and Truxton were awarded silver medals by the Life-Saving Service.

In addition to pulling neophyte swimmers from the surf, members of the Rehoboth Life-Saving Station stood ready to help in other emergencies. In the early years, the resort had no organized fire department, and on December 4, 1893, one of the resort's larger hotels caught fire. The ever-vigilant surfmen spotted the blaze, grabbed several buckets and ran up the beach to help. By the time they arrived, the fire was burning out of control. Other than helping to salvage some of the hotel furniture, there was little the surfmen could do.

Twenty years later, Rehoboth had established a fire department, but when a fire began on Rehoboth Avenue and quickly spread to Baltimore Avenue, the members of the Rehoboth Fire Department were joined by the surfmen from the lifesaving station, and the firefighters worked to control the flames. Before the fire was finally extinguished, the conflagration consumed the Atlantic Hotel, two stores, several houses and several other buildings. On March 1, the board of commissioners for Rehoboth Beach unanimously passed a resolution thanking the surfmen for responding "quickly and nobly" to the emergency.

In 1915, the Life-Saving Service was combined with the Revenue Cutter Service and renamed the United States Coast Guard. Eventually, the Rehoboth Beach station was abandoned, moved to another location and became a private home.

CHAPTER 3

INTO THE TWENTIETH CENTURY

REHOBOTH INHERITS A BOARDWALK

By the start of the twentieth century, Rehoboth Beach had blossomed into a popular resort with several hotels, a number of fine places to eat and a wide sandy beach. During the day, the streets were often crowded with happy vacationers, but after the sun went down there was little to do, and most visitors retreated to their hotel rooms. In 1905, the dark and deserted streets of nighttime Rehoboth were given fresh life with the completion of the town's new boardwalk.

The idea of a boardwalk at Rehoboth originated with a pier built in Brighton, England, in 1823. At that time, Brighton was a popular port for travelers crossing the English Channel. On pleasant days, many Britons spent their leisure time watching the steady stream of passengers on their way to and from France. At Brighton, a "Pleasure Pier" was constructed to serve the passengers boarding the channel boats and the relaxing onlookers. The pleasure pier was built wide enough to accommodate both the constant parade of people and a number of refreshment stands to serve their needs.

A few years later, Dover replaced Brighton as the favorite port for travelers crossing the channel, but Brighton's pier remained in business to serve visitors who continued to come to town to enjoy the sea breezes. The success of the Brighton pier inspired other seacoast towns to build similar structures. At some seaside towns, several pleasure piers were built over the water. When these piers were connected by a wooden walkway that ran parallel to the beach, the seaside boardwalk was born.

When Rehoboth was laid out by the Methodist Camp Meeting Association, Surf Avenue ran along the dunes parallel to the beach. In the beginning, Surf Avenue provided a convenient promenade for people, horses and carriages to take a leisurely stroll, get a good look at the ocean and enjoy the cooling sea breezes. In the 1880s, a boardwalk was

Birds Eye View, Rehoboth, Del.

A few decades after it was established, the resort had developed into a town. *Courtesy of the University of Delaware, Newark, Delaware.*

constructed between Surf Avenue and the beach. The resort's first wooden promenade was just eight feet wide and only a quarter of a mile long.

By the beginning of the twentieth century, more and more vacationers were discovering the joys of the surf. Although most visitors to the resort did not know how to swim, they still enjoyed a dip in the ocean. Their cumbersome bathing suits made movement in the water nearly impossible, and most vacationers spent their time jumping up and down in the surf. Promoters of the resort boasted, "Rehoboth is noted for its safe surf bathing; the beach is clean and free from stones, rough shells, etc., and has no dangerous undertow. Bathing hours are from 11 a.m. until 2 p.m."

At that time, there were no lifeguards on the beach. To provide a measure of safety, a piling was driven into the ocean bottom a few hundred feet offshore, and a safety line was stretched from that piling to a similar post on the beach. Most vacationers remained within a few feet of the safety line while they enjoyed their dip in the surf. After their ocean bath and a change of clothes, visitors to early Rehoboth spent the afternoon strolling the town's streets, boating on the bay or relaxing in the hotel lobby. After the evening meal, there was little to do, and most vacationers went to sleep at an early hour. This changed when a new boardwalk was completed in 1905.

Into the Twentieth Century

The resort's unpaved thoroughfares made it difficult to stroll along the streets of Rehoboth. *Courtesy of the Rehoboth Beach Historical Society.*

The early boardwalk was short, narrow and crowded. *Courtesy of the Rehoboth Beach Historical Society.*

In the early twentieth century, Surf Avenue stood between the boardwalk and the town. *Courtesy of the Rehoboth Beach Historical Society.*

The boardwalk was built on pilings, and it was high enough so that during the day, the shady area under the walkway was popular with those who wished to escape the broiling sun. The boardwalk was an instant success with vacationers, and a promotional brochure entitled *Rehoboth…Queen of Summer Seas!* proclaimed:

> *It is one mile long and sixteen feet wide, with a substantial hand rail, and is lighted by gas the entire length. Here during the season may be found representatives of the wealth, beauty and fashion of our large cities, and while the walk may be crowded, it is always a well-behaved crowd.*

The Rehoboth boardwalk was popular during the day, but after sundown, the new walkway brought a different experience to the resort. The gaslights provided a bright walkway for strolling vacationers who could enjoy the sound of the pounding surf and the refreshing evening breezes. At first, the gaslights were turned off at 11:00 p.m.. Eventually, electric lights were installed, and the boardwalk remained crowded with strollers until the early hours of the morning.

Within a few decades, the boardwalk had become so popular that in 1929 the *Delaware Coast News* reported, "Many people who come to Rehoboth occasionally have wondered why Rehoboth citizens have not made the Boardwalk wider and longer." On some summer days, the boardwalk was thronged with visitors who resolutely marched from one end of the walkway to the other. The steady parade of humanity threatened to choke the boardwalk and stymie what had become the resort's most popular attraction. To avert the crisis on the boards, the Rehoboth Board of Town Commissioners decided to act. According to the *Delaware Coast News*:

As the entire Board heartily approved of the movement to give this resort a boardwalk in keeping with the progress of the resort, the referendum on the questions appears to be only a formality as the majority of the people in the resort are in favor of making the needed repairs and improvements and the extension of the walk to Prospect Street which is in the vicinity of Silver Lake.

Not only would the improved boardwalk be longer, but it would also be widened from twelve to eighteen feet over much of its length, and a section at the foot of Rehoboth Avenue would be thirty-two feet wide. As the *Delaware Coast News* noted, "The action of the town Board in approving the Boardwalk project is just another step in progress which is gradually carrying Rehoboth to the front as one of the attractive resorts along the Atlantic Coast Line."

Most of the resort's residents supported the expansion of the boardwalk. According to the *Delaware Coast News*:

Rehoboth citizens and tax payers who are hoping for increased values in property realize that the appeal which the resort has for city people and the future summer residents of the shore is the ocean, the bathing beach and the boardwalk and they consider money spent to improve these features of Rehoboth is money well spent as it affords more pleasure for the visitors and hence eventually higher value for Rehoboth real estate.

In 1929, the $19,000 spent to upgrade the Rehoboth boardwalk proved to be a sound investment in the town's future. Years later, a visitor to the boardwalk fondly recalled visiting the boardwalk in the 1930s:

After Prohibition was repealed, the state's laws were kind of muddy—and if you had a letter from your parents, you could get into the dance hall. We couldn't drink, but we could go in and dance, which, if you're 16 years old, is a pretty big deal.

The boardwalk had become a permanent fixture at the resort, and it would be difficult to perceive Rehoboth Beach without a boardwalk, even if it were not crowded with "representatives of wealth, beauty and fashion."

THE FIRST CARS RAMBLE INTO TOWN

The car jerked and lurched as it bounced its way through the rutted roads of southern Delaware. In the vehicle was an international entourage of highway engineers that included Ernest Storms of Brussels, Frank Williams of New York and Thomas Aitken of Scotland. As the car's bumpy ride threatened to pitch the engineers from the vehicle, their host, T. Coleman du Pont, seemed to be determined to prove Delaware's reputation as having the worst roads in America. A recent rain had turned the road into a series of potholes and puddles, and when the car splashed through a long, shallow pond, Aitken proclaimed in his Scottish brogue, "And they call this a road! Well, America's a great country, but they've got something to learn about road-making—that they have."

Sometime in the early years of the twentieth century, the soothing, steady sound of the surf was interrupted by the grating sound of a rudimentary gasoline engine. The first horseless carriage had chugged into town. By 1910, cars were becoming commonplace, and some people were becoming

Before cars arrived, Rehoboth Avenue was dominated by the train station in the center of the street. *Courtesy of the University of Delaware, Newark, Delaware.*

Into the Twentieth Century

Some of the first cars had little competition on the streets. *Courtesy of the University of Delaware, Newark, Delaware.*

Early drivers had no problems finding a place to park near the beach. *Courtesy of the Rehoboth Beach Historical Society.*

alarmed at the high speeds that cars were reaching. In some areas, a speed limit of twelve miles per hour was established. In addition, drivers were admonished to "blow horns at crossings." Despite the increasing popularity of cars, the poor state of Delaware's roads made driving to the beach a daunting task.

Many of the roads of Sussex County originated as narrow forest paths that the Native Americans had established long before the first European colonists settled in southern Delaware. As the European settlements grew, the colonists widened the trails, but throughout the nineteenth century, most of Delaware's roads remained unpaved. In wet weather, the state's "highways" became muddy quagmires that made land travel nearly impossible.

At the beginning of the twentieth century, however, beach-bound motorists began bouncing their rickety horseless carriages along the bone-jarring roads. Each trip began with a ritual that had to be observed to the last detail. The grease cups, steering wheel bearings and the brakes were inspected. Oil, water and gas levels were checked. Next, the gear, ignition and air levers were examined to see if they were in working order. The hand throttle was tested. If this proved satisfactory, the ignition process could begin. A few drops of gas were released into a small funnel that hung above the combustion chamber. A knife switch was closed to allow a trickle of electricity to maintain the engine. The throttle could then be opened and the starting crank turned, and the automobile sprang to life.

When the first horseless carriages began to bumble their way toward Rehoboth, many southern Delaware residents got their first glimpse of the newfangled machine as its owner struggled to free it from a boggy rut. Ignoring the derisive cries of "Get a horse!" motorists doggedly continued on with the hope that there would one day be a decent road that led to the beach.

In 1911, Delaware had no statewide highway department to oversee the construction of a modern road system when T. Coleman du Pont announced a proposal that would dramatically change Rehoboth Beach. Although Coleman du Pont was a member of a family that had deep roots in Delaware, he was born in Louisville, Kentucky. After he graduated from the Massachusetts Institute of Technology in 1885, he began a career in the Kentucky coal industry, but he soon moved to Johnstown, Pennsylvania, where du Pont became the general manager of a steel firm. In Johnstown, du Pont became interested in the town's struggling street railway. In 1902, Coleman joined with two of his cousins to take over the family's explosives business, and he moved to Delaware.

After he helped reorganize and diversify the business's holdings, Coleman was able to return to his interest in transportation. In 1911, he made an

Into the Twentieth Century

Before cars, some vehicles in Rehoboth had their own version of a "hybrid" engine. *Courtesy of the University of Delaware, Newark, Delaware.*

extraordinary offer to build the first divided, paved highway from one end of Delaware to the other and to present the highway as his gift to the state. With the determined self-confidence that characterized many members of his family, du Pont assembled a team of highway engineers, bought land for the right of way, gathered a fleet of road-building equipment and hired construction crews. A year after he made the proposal, du Pont and a team of experts were motoring over the rutted roads of southern Delaware, scouting routes for the new highway.

In 1912, Bailey Millard described the work on the Du Pont Highway for the *Technical World Magazine.* According to Millard, lack of detailed maps and difficulty surveying the swampy land of Sussex County caused some of the engineers to complain to du Pont that they were working in the dark, and he suggested, "Why not light it up a bit with skyrockets?"

Millard wrote:

> But it was found on trial that the rockets did not remain long enough in the air to afford sufficient opportunity for the observation. So Mr. Du Pont had heavier rockets brought in, and to these he had parachutes attached, each parachute carrying a light of changing colors and staying up long enough to afford a "sight" from one distant point to another.

Some of the bigger rockets weighed as much as eight pounds apiece, and they provided an effective way of determining the route for the new road. The skyrockets also provided an entertaining pyrotechnic show for the residents along the construction path, but one Sussex County resident was

49

After workers constructed the Du Pont Highway, motorists had an easier time driving to Rehoboth. *Courtesy of the Delaware Public Archives.*

moved to remark, "I should think the time to set off the fireworks would be after the job was done."

After some of the heavy road-building equipment was carried to southern Delaware aboard the Pennsylvania Railroad, the initial section of the road was begun at the state line near Selbyville. The early work on the new road was personally supervised by du Pont, who had a car fitted with a canvas tent to create an early car-camper. According to Millard:

> *As for the motor campwagon, it was a very convenient and comfortable affair. It had large receptacles for instruments and tools and the "wings," as the tent portion of the device was called, were so arranged that they could be spread at a moment's notice whenever the party was overtaken by a storm or wished to camp for the night. I have seen a great many surveying parties in the field, but I have never seen any that had as practicable an outfit as this.*

Despite T. Coleman du Pont's determination, the construction of the road was slowed by Sussex County farmers who believed that he was building the highway to benefit his financial interests. Work on the highway was further slowed by the start of World War I. In 1917, the Delaware State Highway Department was formed, and it assumed control of the construction of the unfinished portions of the highway. Du Pont, however, continued to provide the money for the work. When the Du Pont Highway was completed in 1924, it had cost nearly $4 million.

In 1925, a modern, hard-surfaced road connected the Du Pont Highway to Rehoboth Beach, linking the resort to a modern road network that was known as the Delmarva Trail. A real estate development proclaimed:

> *Just pack up the family in the car and hit the Delmarva Trail. No finer road will be found anywhere in the world than that marvelous ribbon of concrete that stretches its smooth and uninterrupted length from one end of the Diamond State to the other. The Delmarva Trail in an almost unbelievably short time brings you to that garden spot in the State of Delaware, Rehoboth Beach and Rehoboth Heights, Delaware's only seashore resort.*

The Du Pont Highway and other hard-surfaced roads helped transform Rehoboth Beach from a sleepy seaside village into a modern resort. By 1928, so many vacationers drove to Rehoboth in the family car that passenger railroad service to the resort was ended. Although a few open horseless carriages were occasionally spotted in Rehoboth, most of the cars that

REHOBOTH AVENUE LOOKING TOWARDS OCEAN FROM CARLTON HOTEL, REHOBOTH BEACH, DEL.

Cars eventually inundated the town. *Courtesy of the University of Delaware, Newark, Delaware.*

crowded the streets of the resort were newer models whose drivers no longer had to remember to close the knife switch, open the throttle and give the starter a good tug.

VISITORS LEARN TO SWIM

In the early years of the twentieth century, Rehoboth Beach had reached a beachwear crossroads, and some residents were outraged. For years, beach attire had been shrinking, and a number of vacationers were pushing the bounds of good taste and modesty by appearing on the beach dressed in outfits that were scandalously brief. In 1905, the resort's commissioners attempted to restore a degree of decorum to the beach, and they decreed that it was illegal "for any person to bathe in the ocean unless clad in a bathing suit which shall cover the body from the shoulders to the knees." Such suits were to be "of material of suitable texture not to appear vulgar when wet."

In the early years of the resort, ladies who were bold enough to enjoy a dip in the sea wore smock-like bathing gowns that reached to their ankles. Modest ladies sewed weights into the hem of these loose-fitting garments to keep them from floating up and exposing the legs. By the 1890s, women wore black, knee-length wool dresses that featured puffed sleeves and a wide sailor collar. Bloomers were worn under the dress, and no respectable lady appeared on the beach without wearing black stockings, bathing slippers and a hat.

Men did not fare much better. One devotee of the surf recommended that "a man's suit should be of flannel, because that material is both warm and light; it should be made in one piece, sleeveless, reach just to the knee, belted in the waist and above all, close-fitting."

The coverage provided by the early bathing suits ensured that the wearers would not suffer the tanning effects of the sun that would give them a ruddy complexion, which was the mark of a peasant field hand. The abundant material in nineteenth-century bathing attire also guaranteed that few people could actually swim in the ocean. After completing their ocean bath, resort visitors spent the rest of their day strolling the boardwalk, horseback riding or hiking across the sand for a glimpse of the Cape Henlopen Lighthouse. By the beginning of the twentieth century, many beach-goers were interested in more than an ocean bath; they wanted to swim in the ocean. The drive to do more than cling to a rope while being splashed about by the surf was fueled by the Australian swimmer Annette Kellerman.

Into the Twentieth Century

Early devotees of the surf were not dressed for swimming. *Courtesy of the Rehoboth Beach Historical Society.*

In 1904, Kellerman was in England, where she won wide acclaim for a demanding seventeen-mile swim along the River Thames. She wore a form-fitting suit that was a radical departure from Victorian bathing attire. She once commented, "I can't swim wearing more stuff than you hang on a clothesline."

On American beaches, women followed Kellerman's example, and they began to wear bathing suits that exposed the legs and arms to give them the freedom of movement needed to swim in the ocean. This public affront to modesty led to the arrests of some women as soon as they appeared on the beach, while others were dragged forcibly from the surf. When a woman on a New Jersey beach wore a bathing suit that exposed part of her thigh, she was attacked by an outraged mob. In Delaware, the Rehoboth town leaders were content with their decree that bathing attire must "cover the body from the shoulders to the knees." By the time that the United States entered World War I, bathing attire had dwindled to the point that the American Association of Park Superintendents was moved to issue "Bathing Suit Regulations" in an effort to delineate the limits of modesty. In general, the regulations decreed: "No all white or flesh colored suits permitted, nor suits that expose the chest lower than a line drawn on a level with the arm pits." For women, the association declared:

"MAKE FAST SARAH!"

THE Surf Bathing is delightful, the atmosphere bracing, and the excellent amusements makes this resort an ideal one for those who desire REST, HEALTH and PLEASURE.

Rehoboth Beach Del.

WHERE PINE FOREST AND OCEAN MEET

Send six cent stamps for summer book to T.MURDOCH,G.P.A. Md.,Del.&Va.Ry.Co. Pier No. 2, Light Street

Vacationers were urged to take the plunge into the surf. *Courtesy of the Rehoboth Beach Historical Society.*

> *Blouse and bloomer suits may be worn with or without stockings, provided the blouse has quarter-arm sleeves or close-fitting arm-holes, and provided bloomers are full and not shorter than four inches above the knee (top of patella). Jersey suits may be worn with or without stockings, provided the suit has a skirt or skirt effect, with quarter-arm sleeves or close-fitting arm holes and trunks not shorter than four inches above the knee, and the bottom of the skirt must be shorter than two inches above the bottom of the trunks.*

For men, the association decreed:

> *Men's suits must have skirt effect, or shirt worn outside of trunks, except when flannel knee pants with belt and fly front are worn. The trunks must not be shorter than four inches above the knee (top of patella) and the skirt must not be shorter than two inches above the bottom of the trunks.*

Despite the association's promulgation, bathing suits for both men and women continued to shrink. When American soldiers returned home after World War I, they reported that women on French beaches frolicked in the surf without wearing hats or stockings, and during the 1920s, these items dropped out of most American beach-goers' ensembles. On the beach, both

54

In the early twentieth century, most beach-goers visited the sand fully clothed. *Courtesy of the Rehoboth Beach Historical Society.*

Distinctive "roundhouses" gave people a good view of the surf without getting sand in their shoes. *Courtesy of the Rehoboth Beach Historical Society.*

men and women appeared in modern bathing suits that allowed them to swim freely in the ocean. By the end of the decade, some males appeared on Delaware beaches without wearing shirts with their bathing trunks. This so scandalized some Rehoboth residents that the town commissioners of Rehoboth continued to promulgate orders mandating the arrest of any male who did not wear a shirt on the beach, but bathing suits continued to evolve into more revealing beach attire.

GUNNERS ON THE BAY

During the late nineteenth century, vacationers climbed aboard trains for a pleasant ride to Rehoboth Beach, and as they hustled to their seats, they were sometimes greeted by passengers toting guns, decoys and other hunting paraphernalia. During the years after the Civil War, when many vacationers were just discovering the joys of the Delaware beaches, hunting for waterfowl on the coastal bays was a popular pastime that had attracted people to the coastal area for generations.

In the coastal region, sportsmen hunted black duck, widgeon, teal, mallard, geese and other birds. In addition to those who hunted the waterfowl for pleasure, commercial hunters also shot many of the same types of birds, which they sold to markets in Wilmington and Philadelphia.

Hunting wild ducks was not an easy task. Unlike geese, which had a reputation for stupidity, ducks were clever animals that were alert to any changes in the landscape. Hunters had to spend time in the coastal marshes lying on their backs on the soggy ground or in a "Sink Boat," whose sides were nearly level with the water's edge. The small boat had just enough room for a prone hunter to lie in wait for the game. Some hunters dug holes in the dunes and waited in this sandy burrow for hours until their prey arrived. In addition, the wildfowl were more numerous in the fall and spring when the weather was often damp and cold.

Writing in *Scribner's Magazine* a few years after the resort was established, T. Robinson Warren commented:

> *As the weather becomes colder, and the ice begins to form, the fowl seek the southern waters, some going direct, and others gradually working down through the bays on the coast of Delaware, Virginia, and North Carolina. Just to the south-west of Cape Henlopen, there is fine shooting in Rehoboth Bay, which, although accessible, is not much frequented by gunners.*

Into the Twentieth Century

As Warren pointed out, the coastal bays, such as Rehoboth Bay, were very shallow and had been abandoned by all but the smallest vessels. These conditions attracted a variety of wildfowl that stopped along the Delaware coast during their annual migration to and from the breeding places in the far north. In addition, Rehoboth Bay was used as a feeding grounds and resting place for countless thousands of ducks and geese that migrated along the coast each spring and fall.

In 1882, *A Paradise for Gunners and Anglers*, a guidebook for sportsmen, found that the beach at Rehoboth was

> *hard and solid,* [and] *can be traversed with safety and comfort on foot or in carriage from Cape Henlopen to Indian River, a continuous distance of from ten to twelve miles…Water of the finest quality can be obtained from wells sunk almost anywhere in the vicinity, to a depth of from ten to fifteen feet. The land adjacent is considerably higher than the level of the tides, affording a magnificent view of the ocean. It is of course dry, and therefore malaria has never been known to prevail there.*

In the early twentieth century, the interest in wildfowl hunting along the Delaware coast declined. The number of hunters who visited Rehoboth was vastly overshadowed by the horde of vacationers who descended on the resort each summer, but a dedicated number of sportsmen continued to visit the coastal bays each winter. In 1931, an observer reported:

> *The season for shooting wild ducks, geese, coots, snipe, brant and gallinules throughout lower Delaware will soon open and sportsmen are prepared to take to the inland waterways and shore bays, which are most frequented by these game birds. Owing to the very warm weather, gunners fear they will not have much success because so far the birds are keeping well away from the feeding grounds near the shore.*

Conservation laws and other restrictions on hunting led to a decline in the sport in the Rehoboth area. Today, most of the vacationers who stalk the wildfowl of the Delaware coast shoot the birds with a camera.

FIRING OFF THE COAST

In June 1914, vacationers were enjoying another pleasant summer, but in Europe, an assassin's bullet felled Archduke Francis Ferdinand of Austria

During World War I, storms drove the *Merrimac* and the *Severn* onto the beach. *Courtesy of the Delaware Public Archives.*

and initiated a chain of events that led to World War I. In August 1914, the United States was officially neutral, but some residents of Rehoboth turned an anxious glance toward the Atlantic and the conflict that was raging on the other side of the ocean. Two decades earlier, when the United States had declared war against Spain in 1898, resort residents had realized that enemy warships could steam over the horizon at any time. No enemy ships appeared off the Delaware coast during the Spanish-American War, but the development of long-range naval guns, submarines and airplanes presented new threats to Rehoboth.

Days after World War I began in Europe, the steamship *Brandenberg* sat quietly at its dock in Philadelphia as the crew of the German passenger vessel worked to load coal, foodstuffs and other materials. The stevedores stuffed cargo into spaces normally reserved for the sixteen hundred passengers the vessel usually carried.

The crew of the *Brandenberg* rushed to get to sea before the American government detained all vessels that belonged to the warring powers for the duration of the war. According to a report by the *New York Times*:

> *Her hold and bunkers, and even the staterooms were loaded with coal, and every available space between decks contained supplies of foodstuffs. The character of the steamer's cargo led many to believe that she would attempt to transfer the coal and provisions to a German battleship at sea, but this was denied by both the Captain of the vessel and the German Consul here.*

Into the Twentieth Century

While the *Brandenberg* was being loaded at Philadelphia, Rehoboth Beach was completing a surprisingly successful summer season. Early in the year, a strong nor'easter had bulldozed its way up the Delaware coast and plowed into Rehoboth Beach. The ocean surged through a one-thousand-foot-wide stream to the bay, and flooding water carried away any structures in its path. In addition, the waves had carried away more than two hundred feet of the boardwalk and damaged a number of homes on Surf Avenue. There was so much wreckage in the resort that people doubted that Rehoboth could be ready to receive vacationers when the summer season began. After several months of demanding work, the debris from the storm was removed and most of the damage was repaired. During 1914, vacationers returned to Rehoboth to enjoy the refreshing surf, the cool ocean breeze and the rebuilt boardwalk.

The news of the outbreak of war in Europe failed to discourage vacationers from crowding into Rehoboth during the last week in August for a final summer fling. Reports of English warships off the Delaware coast added to the excitement, and when the *Brandenberg* had sailed from Philadelphia, many eager eyes began to watch the horizon for some sign of the naval confrontation.

About two o'clock in the morning on August 27, those who were enjoying a late-night stroll on the boardwalk saw flashes of light near the horizon. Moments later, they heard the low rumbling sounds that were assumed to be the distant echoes of firing cannons. As reports of the firing off Rehoboth Beach spread, more people gathered on the boardwalk, and they strained to get a glimpse of the action. According to the *New York Times*:

> *Vivid flashes accompanied by rumbling aroused the people living near Cape Henlopen this morning...It is supposed that the firing was by a cruiser...The noise and the flashes were first observed about 2 o'clock. On the boardwalk at Rehoboth a crowd watched. The firing continued until about 5 o'clock, when there were reflections as if two boats were on fire. No more was heard and when daylight broke, nothing was seen to indicate a fight. English and German cruisers have been seen off the coast here, apparently watching for ships to come out of Philadelphia.*

When the sun came up, a piece of a spar and part of the bow of a boat were retrieved from the beach. Many in the resort believed that they had witnessed the distant sights and sounds of a sea battle. There were reports that the British had captured the *Brandenberg*, but the German passenger ship had sailed down the Delaware Bay without difficulty. After the *Brandenberg* reached Cape Henlopen, the German vessel continued into the Atlantic. Although it was reported that there were several British warships lurking in international waters that began three miles offshore, the *Brandenberg* was able to cross the ocean unmolested.

As the war raged in Europe, the United States government attempted to deal with the country's antiquated coastal defense system by combining the Revenue Cutter Service with the Life-Saving Service to create the United States Coast Guard. After the merger was completed in 1915, the surfmen at the Rehoboth Life-Saving Station were replaced by an armed Coast Guard crew who were prepared to save lives and to defend the beach from enemy invaders.

While these changes were taking place, vacationers were able to enjoy a few more peaceful summers at Rehoboth, but in April 1917, the United States declared war on Germany. With the American entry into World War I, the prospect that Rehoboth and the coastal region would be attacked became real. To help defend southern Delaware, the Naval Coast Reserve recruited volunteers to serve on minelayers, submarine chasers, patrol boats and minesweepers. In addition, members of the reserve were employed onshore as signalmen and lookouts, as well as assigned other shore duties.

In April 1918, the steam tug *Eastern* struggled though a storm with two barges, the *Merrimac* and the *Severn*, in tow. As the *Eastern* struggled to maintain headway in the heavy ocean swells, the wind continued to blow the steam tug and its two barges toward the Delaware beach. It is not known if wartime shipping practices caused the *Eastern* to sail closer to the coast than normal, but it soon became evident that the three vessels were dangerously close to the beach. Under normal circumstances, the *Eastern* should have been able to turn and steam out to sea, but the winds continued to drive the steam tug, the *Merrimac* and the *Severn* toward the shore.

As the three vessels approached the beach, the crew of the *Eastern* cut the lines that bound the tug to the *Merrimac* and the *Severn*. Freed of the barges that were dragging it toward shore, the tug was able to power out to deeper water. The wind, however, continued to propel the *Merrimac* and the *Severn* toward the shore, and the two barges did not stop until they ran aground on the beach.

The *Merrimac* came to rest in front of St. Agnes by the Sea, which was maintained by the Franciscan Sisters as a home for nuns who taught in the Delaware Catholic schools. The 640-ton *Merrimac* had sustained significant damage, and the barge began to settle into the sand at the end of Brooklyn Avenue. The *Severn*, on the other hand, appeared unscathed as it slid to a stop on the beach.

Into the Twentieth Century

The storm that forced the *Merrimac* and the *Severn* onto the sand also ripped parts of the boardwalk apart. *Courtesy of the Delaware Public Archives.*

After the storm subsided, tugs were able to float the *Severn* off the beach, but the *Merrimac* was in such poor shape and so deeply trapped in the sand that it was not possible to extradite the barge from the beach. After wreckers had salvaged what they could from the *Merrimac*, the remains of the barge were left to settle in the Rehoboth sand.

A few months after the *Merrimac* became a permanent fixture in the sands of Rehoboth, the *U-117*, a mine-laying German submarine, arrived off the coast. The enemy sub was able to cruise along the beach without being seen. During World War I, German submarines made headlines by torpedoing surface ships, but during the summer of 1918, the *U-117* was on a mission to plant a minefield off the Delaware coast.

The deadly minefield had been in place for nearly a month when the USS *Minnesota* steamed southward past Rehoboth Beach. The 450-foot-long *Minnesota* was one of America's most modern battleships, and its large, twelve-inch guns could blow most other vessels out of the water. By September 1918, the deadlock of war that had gripped Europe for three years was finally breaking, and some were predicting that the fighting would be over in a matter of weeks.

As the *Minnesota* blithely sailed southward on September 29, 1918, the warship struck one of the mines left by the *U-117*. The exploding mine tore a large hole in the *Minnesota*'s hull, and the sea began to flood the battleship.

61

The American sailors aboard the warship quickly closed and locked the *Minnesota*'s hatches. The battleship was severely damaged, but the prompt action of the crew saved the ship. With the flooding stabilized, the battleship headed northward past Rehoboth to Philadelphia for repairs.

Several days later, the cargo ship *Saetia* entered the minefield off Fenwick Island. When the cargo vessel encountered a German mine, a blast ripped the ship apart. Minutes after the blast, the *Saetia* disappeared beneath the waves, but the ship's crewmen were rescued by the Coast Guard.

The damage to the *Minnesota* and the destruction of the *Saetia* in the last days of World War I showed that Rehoboth Beach would be on the front lines of a world war. When the United States entered the Second World War in 1941, the fear of submarine attacks in the waters off the Delaware coast became a reality.

CHAPTER 4

REHOBOTH ROARS
IN THE 1920S

BOOMTOWN ON THE COAST

When the real estate developer Henry Conant arrived in Rehoboth in the early 1920s, he had to pass over a canal to reach the resort. In 1913, a canal that connected Lewes Creek with Rehoboth Bay had been constructed to enable boats to skirt behind Cape Henlopen and reach the coastal bays without venturing into the Atlantic Ocean. Most of the commercial traffic in the canal consisted of motorboats that towed barges of tomatoes from landings on Indian River and Rehoboth Bay to a cannery west of the resort.

The canal, however, acted like a moat between Rehoboth and the mainland, and the waterway helped to reduce the number of free-roaming animals loose in the resort. When Rehoboth Beach was established, animals were very much a part of the resort. Vacationers rode horses on the beach, horses and oxen pulled carriages and carts through the town's streets and cattle grazed on open plots of land that were common in the early years of the resort. But other animals were not allowed this freedom. Pigs, poultry and other livestock that provided fresh food for the resort's visitors were kept in pens scattered about town.

In 1905, the town commissioners had attempted to reduce the number of animals wandering the streets of Rehoboth by making it illegal for "any horse, gelding, mule, cow, sheep, hogs, goats, or other cattle whatever" to run loose in the resort. In addition, the commissioners declared it illegal to erect "any privy, pigpen or other appurtenances generally considered obnoxious and unwholesome."

When Conant arrived in Rehoboth, horse-drawn carriages were still a major mode of transportation, but he saw that modern roads would soon reach Rehoboth. When people could drive over hard-surfaced roads to the resort, the town would boom. In the Roaring Twenties, many people believed that there should be a chicken in every pot, a car in the garage and a place at the beach, and Conant decided that Rehoboth Beach was ready for a major expansion.

The Grand Bridge, Rehoboth Beach, Del.

Left: As the Roaring Twenties began, a single bridge crossed the canal. *Courtesy of the University of Delaware, Newark, Delaware.*

Below: As the town expanded, Rehoboth moved southward. *Courtesy of the Rehoboth Beach Historical Society.*

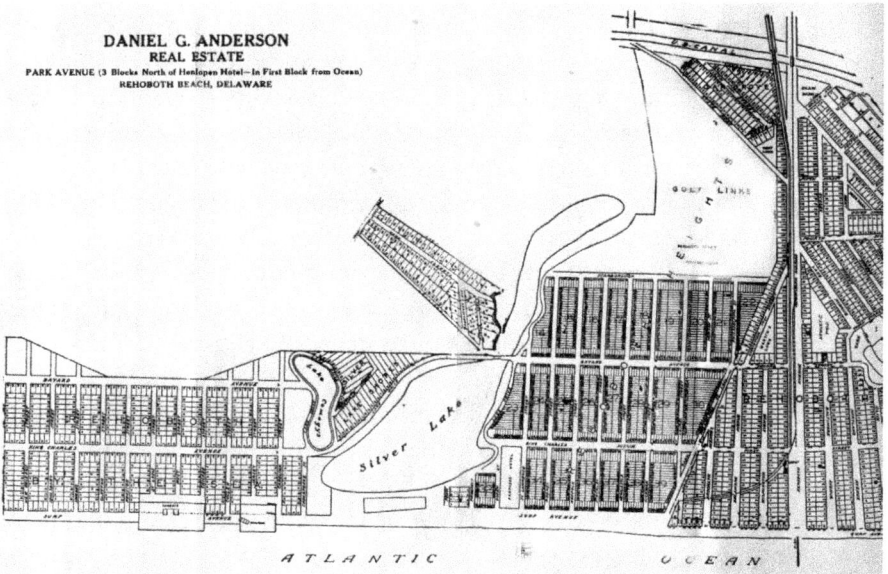

DANIEL G. ANDERSON
REAL ESTATE
PARK AVENUE (3 Blocks North of Henlopen Hotel—In First Block from Ocean)
REHOBOTH BEACH, DELAWARE

Rehoboth Roars in the 1920s

In 1923, Conant bought 150 acres of land on the south side of town. His tract lay between Philadelphia Street and Silver Lake, and it stretched from the beach to the planned Rehoboth Beach Country Club, next to the Lewes and Rehoboth Canal. The Conant development sat on elevated land that promised homeowners excellent views of Silver Lake and the Atlantic Ocean. The developer divided the wooded tract into lots, laid out streets and sidewalks and planned for the installation of water lines and electric service. Conant dubbed his development Rehoboth Heights and urged prospective buyers to

> *picture yourself in a summer vacation spot amid pleasant shades at the edge of the lake and ocean in the clear deep waters of which many a good fry disports himself, ignorant of the mission he is to perform for you, your family and friends at your cottage table—where the summer sun warms an expanse of sandy beach that has no superior along the Atlantic Coast—where vast stretches of pine woods allure your steps with their depth and solitude.*

In his promotional literature, Conant touted the advantages of owning a place at the beach:

> *If you have always wanted a summer cottage by the sea—here is your opportunity; if you want to invest your money in property that is as safe and true as any seaside resort that can be found anywhere here is your opportunity!*

For those who needed an added incentive to buy, Conant, who was from Chincoteague, Virginia, entered purchasers into a lottery whose main prize was a pony.

Conant priced his fifty- by one-hundred-foot lots from $400 to $1,000. Buyers were required to put 20 percent down, and they paid 5 percent a month on the remaining balance. Conant assured buyers that their investment was an economically sound one:

> *Rehoboth Beach is growing and expanding; Rehoboth Heights is part of that expansion. The lots in Rehoboth Heights are offered at an unusually low price. It is safe to predict that they will be worth twice as much in less than two years.*

Two years after Conant began selling lots in Rehoboth Heights, the road from Georgetown to the resort was paved, and a drawbridge was constructed over the canal. When he began to market Rehoboth Heights, Delaware's road network was blossoming, and Conant urged vacationers to use the Delmarva Trail to reach the resort. Conant's development quickly sold out. In 1926, the Eastern Shore Gas & Electric Company was chartered to provide electricity to Rehoboth Beach, and in the same year, Rehoboth Heights was annexed to the town.

Conant had promised that lots in the development would quickly double their value. Before the end of the decade, lots in Rehoboth were going for between $1,700 and $2,100. Those who had hit the Delmarva Trail and purchased a lot in Rehoboth Heights had bought a place in one of America's finest resorts, and they had made a spectacularly profitable investment.

Rehoboth was still booming in 1928, when Lieutenant Governor J. Hall Anderson, who was also a summer resident of the resort and a member of the town commission, made the official address to open the summer season. The *Delaware Coast News* reported:

> [He] *gave a very delightful address on the progress made by Rehoboth during the past few years. During the course of his talk he requested the local people to have pride in their town, to cooperate with those who were spending money to beautify the resort, and to meet such efforts on the part of outside citizens by accomplishing things among ourselves.*

Anderson also praised the opening of the new Dolle Recreation Hall, which he believed was an indication of the high caliber of the new businesses that were being built along the boardwalk. According to the *Delaware Coast News*:

Visitors were now dressed to swim in the ocean. *Courtesy of the Delaware Public Archives.*

Rehoboth Roars in the 1920s

Some vacationers were still reluctant to dive into the surf. *Courtesy of the Delaware Public Archives.*

> *The Dolle Hall was opened with our mayor, Mr. Wingate, throwing the first ball down the bowling alley. Contrary to expectations, he knocked down 7 pins and was applauded vigorously. Mr. George Burks, who will have charge of the alleys bowled a game of duck pins and Mr. Wingate suffered defeat by a score of 79 to 69.*

In March 1929, the *Delaware Coast News* was optimistic about the years ahead:

> *Rehoboth's growth depends on the man and his family that is interested enough in the seashore to build his summer home and stay here during the summer season. A large percentage of the cottage owners in this resort occupy their own cottages and this speaks well for the future of this resort. The natural beauties of Rehoboth, its peace and quietude have a tendency to make this resort a family gathering place. The noise, hustle and bustle of the average seacoast resort is missing in Rehoboth, and yet there [are] many various ways and means for amusements.*

FORE!

When Henry Conant began developing Rehoboth Heights, he promised that homeowners would have access to a variety of seaside amenities that included:

Boating—An incomparable beach along the Atlantic Ocean where thousands of people every year are invigorated with salt water bathing.
Fishing—There is perhaps no finer fishing grounds along the Atlantic Coast.
Entertainment—Various amusements including attractive commodious movie houses showing the best pictures every day.

In addition, Conant promised that residents of Rehoboth Heights could enjoy "Golf—Preparations are now underway for the erection of a Country Club and Golf Course."

While the Dutch colonists were busy establishing settlements in Delaware, the rules of golf were being standardized in Scotland. Some of the early courses were set up on the rolling, grass-covered dunes that separated the sandy beaches along the coast from the more usable pastureland. These dunes were known as "Link Land," and they were ancestors of the term "links" for a golf course.

Along the Delaware coast, there was plenty of link land to establish golf courses, but the residents of Sussex County had no time to chase a little white ball over the coastal countryside. Toward the end of the nineteenth century, the golf bug finally began to bite in America. In 1894, *Scribner's Magazine* reported, "Golf has been threatening to cross the seas these last five years. It came unobtrusively, and this year has fairly taken root and spread itself." In 1895, there were fewer than one hundred golf courses in America; five years later, there were nearly one thousand. But when Conant arrived in Rehoboth during the 1920s, there were no first-class golf courses in the coastal region. With the sales of lots in Rehoboth Heights moving at a brisk pace, Conant lost no time in constructing the promised golf course. After the course was completed, the Rehoboth Beach Country Club took great pride in getting the links ready for players by the beginning of the summer beach season.

In 1926, the *Delaware Coast News* reported:

The golf course is in very good shape at the present time and many members of the club are taking advantage of the pleasant days. The Fairways have all received top dressings and have been rolled several times and there are new tees on the 2nd, 5th, and 6th holes.

In addition to conducting its own tournaments, the Rehoboth Beach County Club also fielded a golf team that played in a league of clubs on the Delmarva Peninsula.

At the same time, the newspaper contained an enthusiastic advertisement for a matched set of Robertson's golf clubs. "The Heads!" the ad proclaimed, were made of "hand forged steel." The shafts were made of "natural white second growth air seasoned hickory," and the grips were finished with "impregnated calfskin." The entire set could be had for only twenty dollars.

Over the years, additional courses have been established in the vicinity of Rehoboth, and for many people, a round of golf has become just as much a part of a visit to the beach as a dip in the surf or a stroll along the boardwalk. What *Scribner's Magazine* had predicted over a century ago has come true: "Once seen golf cannot be forgotten; once experienced, it will not be neglected. It has fairly got us now, and it may be trusted to keep us."

HAVE A DRINK ON THE WCTU

When the Methodist Camp Meeting Association founded Rehoboth, the movement to outlaw alcoholic beverages was steadily gaining strength. In colonial times, Americans consumed a vast quantity of wine, liquor and other alcoholic drinks with lively names, such as Cherry Bounce, Flip and

Strollers on the boardwalk stop to have a drink on the WCTU. *Courtesy of the Delaware Public Archives.*

Syllabub. The resulting drunkenness was blamed for poverty, crime and a host of other social ills. The abuse of alcohol led to a drive to prohibit the sale and consumption of all alcoholic beverages, and when Rehoboth was established, the association banned alcoholic beverages in the resort. Within a few years, however, the ban was lifted.

In 1874, a year after the resort was established, the Woman's Christian Temperance Union, known as the WCTU, was organized to promote total abstinence from alcohol, tobacco and all harmful drugs. The WCTU and other organizations were able to generate such support for the prohibition of alcoholic beverages that, in 1919, the Eighteenth Amendment to the federal Constitution outlawed the manufacture, sale or transportation of intoxicating liquors.

During Prohibition, shipments of illegal alcohol were loaded aboard small vessels in Canadian ports. Whiskey, gin and other alcoholic spirits were placed in rectangular metal containers that could be easily stacked on a boat. Often, the metal tins were covered with a cloth sack so that they could be handled quietly. The cloth covering also prevented the tins from reflecting light that would alert the revenue agents to the bootlegger's presence.

Once loaded, the boat would leave Canadian waters and sail down the East Coast. Some of the rumrunners stopped offshore of the Delaware coast, where they were met by small boats. The illegal booze was loaded aboard the boats for the run through the surf to the beach. Once ashore, the bootleg liquor was reloaded onto trucks and driven to speakeasies in Philadelphia, Baltimore and other cities.

Throughout the 1920s, the Coast Guard patrolled Delaware waters to squash the landing of illegal liquor, and in 1923, Captain A.J. Henderson, the commandant of the Coast Guard's Sixth District (which included Rehoboth), issued special orders to his men to be particularly vigilant along the Delaware coast. Despite these efforts, the rumrunners often avoided detection. Although rumrunners cruised the waters off Rehoboth regularly, most avoided landing too close to the resort. Not only were the members of the Coast Guard station on alert, but the bootleggers also preferred to work in the shadows, and Rehoboth had developed too much for them to be sure that no one was watching as they unloaded their illegal cargo.

The Coast Guard made a number of significant stops along the coast, but it had to deal with the leniency of the Delaware courts. Once, when a group of bootleggers was caught red-handed with the liquor piled next to them on the beach, they were released because it could not be shown that the booze was theirs.

Rehoboth Roars in the 1920s

Although Prohibition outlawed alcohol, the members of the Rehoboth WCTU continued to lobby against the evils of alcohol. In April 1929, the group sponsored a cafeteria-style lunch at the Epworth Methodist Episcopal Church. The menu included meatloaf, waffles, hot rolls, deviled eggs, potato salad, pickles, cake and pie. The money raised by the lunch helped defer the cost of a drinking fountain that was erected later that year at the end of Rehoboth Avenue and the boardwalk.

By the end of the decade, it was obvious that the noble experiment of Prohibition lacked public support and had spawned a number of other problems. After Prohibition was repealed, alcohol returned to the beach, but the stone arch of the fountain erected by the dedicated women of the WCTU has become a fixture at Rehoboth.

END OF THE LIGHTHOUSE

Writing in 1890 for *Scribner's Magazine*, John R. Spears stated:

> *Indeed no beacons in the world excite stronger or more conflicting emotions in the breast of the mariner than the black-spiraled tower and flashing white light of Hatteras, and the plain white shaft and steady glare of Henlopen.*

The Delaware lighthouse was one of the most recognizable features on the American coast, and it provided an added attraction for vacationers at Rehoboth. The lighthouse, however, was built on sand.

Built a decade before the American Revolution, the Cape Henlopen Lighthouse sat on one of the high dunes of the cape. When the first European colonists arrived along the coast, they discovered a great sandy ridge that ran along the northern side of the cape. In the eighteenth century, the dune that crowned Cape Henlopen was more than seventy feet high and nearly two miles long. The base of this ridge of sand was washed by the waves, but the sand was held firmly in place by the twisted pine trees and coarse grasses that were deeply rooted in the dune and promised to anchor the sand permanently. When the eight-sided tower was finished, the lighthouse sat securely on its lofty perch on the top of the dunes, far from the pounding surf.

The tower's distinctive shape and bright beacon guided mariners into Delaware Bay for over a century and a half, and when Rehoboth became a summer resort, the sight of the tower was a magnet that some vacationers could not ignore. "Rehoboth Beach," a promoter of the resort wrote in the early twentieth century, "is fortunate in possessing a very good boardwalk,

A hike to see the Cape Henlopen Lighthouse was a highlight of the afternoon. *Courtesy of the Lewes Historical Society.*

trending the beach for quite a distance, where the summering folks may stroll to their heart's content." Other ocean resorts also had boardwalks, but Rehoboth had an attraction that was different: "When one walks to the northernmost end he can plainly see silhouetted against the sky in the distance the gray outline of the Cape Henlopen Lighthouse."

As a resort booster commented:

> *If one be a little venturesome, he will doubtless want to tramp along the beach to where the lighthouse stands, and if there be two or three or more in the party, it will no doubt appear to be a sure-enough lark; but the distance from the upper end of the boardwalk is very much further than it looks, and unless the pedestrians in this case are rather better walkers than most people, they will probably be "Weary Willies" of a pronounced type when they return. The writer started on this same tramp one lovely summer's day, but he was well pleased to return before he reached the halfway point.*

Rehoboth Roars in the 1920s

By 1926, the sand was quickly eroding from the base of the lighthouse. *Courtesy of the Delaware Public Archives.*

In the years before the automobile had driven all of the animals from the resort, many people knew how to ride, and there were livery stables in town:

> *As horses and ponies are obtainable at the Rehoboth stables, the proper, profitable, and pleasurable thing to do is to hire an animal and visit the lighthouse on horseback. It is worth while. And aside from the interest that attaches to the lighthouse, the gallop along the long stretch of sandy beach, with old ocean beating away almost at your feet, is thrilling and well worth the time and slight expense.*

By the 1920s, however, an ominous development had taken place at the dunes supporting the lighthouse. The steady westward drift of the beach had eroded much of the sand between the beach and the beacon, and the lighthouse now perched on the edge of a sandy bluff. On April 13, 1926, the inevitable happened and the venerable lighthouse tumbled onto the beach. Immediately after the tower collapsed, coastal residents rushed to the beach to pick through the rubble for a relic of the old tower. While many long-term residents of Rehoboth lamented the demise of the lighthouse, others were busy enjoying the boom that engulfed the resort during the Roaring Twenties.

ARTISTS PAINT THE TOWN

In 1878, Ethel Pennewill Brown was born in Wilmington. It would be decades before Ethel would arrive in Rehoboth, but her arrival would change the resort in a unique way. Jann Gilmore, in her study of Brown published in a special double issue of the journal *Delaware History*, noted that at the age of sixteen, Ethel knew she wanted to be a serious artist. As her aunt, Rose Virden, put it, "Anybody can cook, but very few have the talent that you have for drawing and painting." Virden was a Rehoboth property owner, and it may have been about this time that Ethel first visited the Delaware resort. Fueled by the prosperity of the Roaring Twenties, the resort was bulging at the seams with a number of fine hotels, a wide boardwalk and several dozen blocks of beach homes and cottages.

After she completed her artistic training under Howard Pyle, Ethel decided that the clean, bright air of Rehoboth made the resort the ideal place for her to paint. During World War I, Brown purchased a lot on Columbia Avenue, just north of the center of town, and cleared the land for a house. At first, she spent summers at the resort, but eventually she became a full-time resident of Rehoboth.

Rehoboth Roars in the 1920s

In 1922, Ethel married William Leach, whom she had met when they were both young artists. Will lacked Ethel's intense desire to paint. Will would spend the majority of his time maintaining the modest rental properties that the couple acquired in Rehoboth, while Ethel's success as an artist continued to blossom. In 1923, she won the silver ribbon at the Pennsylvania Academy of the Fine Arts for *Pilot Town—Lewes*. During this time, Ethel and Will often exhibited their work in the resort, and they both saw the need for a way for local artists to be recognized.

The Cape Henlopen Lighthouse was one of the couple's favorite subjects, and they painted it often. Ethel once wrote:

> *At low tide, we walked or drove along the sands—past the wreck, the smaller dunes—the Life Saving Station. On again until we came to the great dune and the Old Henlopen Light! Whether rainy day or clouds scudding across the sky—making cloud-shadow, or else a hot day with the sun beating mercilessly down, we were always thrilled with what met our gaze.*

When the lighthouse collapsed in 1926, Will Leach was one of the first to reach the fallen tower. He retrieved the door and a number of other objects from the rubble that was strewn across the beach. The Leaches proudly displayed the lighthouse door in their Rehoboth home for many years, and eventually they donated it to the Zwaanendael Museum in Lewes.

While visiting other vacation areas, Ethel had noticed that many resorts hosted thriving art exhibitions. In 1928, she founded the Annual Summer Art Exhibitions at the Village Improvement Association in Rehoboth Beach. Colonel Wilber Sherman Corkran arrived in Rehoboth Beach. Corkran was an experienced developer who spotted the potential of the Dodd Farm, the site of Peter Marsh's old house on the northern edge of the resort.

The property was a prime piece of land that extended from west of the Lewes and Rehoboth Canal to the Atlantic Ocean, and after Corkran had purchased the land, he announced that the two hundred acres would be developed into a residential park named Henlopen Acres. Corkran divided the Dodd Farm into lots, built a yacht basin and filled in the lowland known as the Old Salt Lake to create additional lots. Henlopen Acres featured winding roads, bridle paths and children's playgrounds that were tastefully placed so that some of the mature pine and oak groves on the Dodd Farm were left undisturbed. In addition, Corkran located the utility lines below ground, and the landscaping was designed and maintained in a natural manner. Architecturally, the colonel wanted the buildings to reflect the low, rambling farmhouses of colonial America. These homes featured wide porches and outbuildings that were attached to the main structure by covered passageways.

The centerpiece of Henlopen Acres was Peter Marsh's old house, the Homestead, where Corkran and his wife, Louise, continued to live. Working with Ethel, they turned Peter Marsh's old house into a center for the arts. In addition to hosting flower and art shows, Mrs. Corkran initiated Old Sussex Days, which celebrated the history of the coastal region. In 1938, the Rehoboth Art League was established, and Ethel was named a life member, honorary president and a member of the league's advisory board.

Following World War II, Rehoboth Beach continued to grow, and the quiet seaside town that had once captivated Ethel began to slide into the past. In 1957, Will passed away, but Ethel continued to paint. She finished her last work, *The Woodland Ferry*, shortly before her death on December 30, 1959. Ethel P. Brown Leach, however, had brought an artistic presence to Rehoboth that made the Delaware resort unique.

CHAPTER 5

REHOBOTH SURVIVES
THE 1930S

FLIERS PUT ON A SHOW

Harold White vividly remembers the day when he climbed into the seat for his first ride in an airplane. During the Roaring Twenties, open-seat biplanes zoomed above attentive crowds as daredevils hung by their hands, walked on the wings and performed other death-defying stunts. Like most ten-year-olds, White was electrified by the sight of a plane flying high over Delaware, but when young Harold first climbed into the open seat of a WACO biplane, he had the added thrill of taking to the air in a plane piloted by his father, Jack.

During the 1920s, Jack White was one of a small cadre of licensed pilots in Delaware, and admiring crowds watched Jack flying high over the sands of Rehoboth Beach. At that time, an airplane parked on the edge of a nearby field attracted the attention of passersby; two planes parked together drew a crowd. According to his son Harold:

> [Jack] *became involved, as most young aviators would, by barnstorming and participating in air shows, racing around the pylons, training young students, taking up passengers, and risking the sands of Rehoboth Beach as a landing strip.*

In July 1929, a contemporary of Jack White, Captain Forrest Wenyon, flew his biplane high over Rehoboth while a crowd of beach-goers watched as a small blizzard of paper leaflets spewed from his aircraft. As the papers fluttered to the ground, they were snatched up by the vacationers, who discovered that on Sunday, July 14, there would be a parachute jump "by the boy who laughs at death—the one and only smiling Mickey Efferson" within sight of the Rehoboth boardwalk.

Mickey Efferson relaxes a few years after he was the boy who laughed at death. *Courtesy of the Delaware Public Archives.*

When Mickey Efferson, the self-styled "Dare-Devil of the Air," arrived over Rehoboth, the boardwalk was packed with vacationers eager to see the daredevil leap from the plane. According to the *Delaware Coast News*:

> *Many thousands of people were lined up against the railing to see F.P. Wenyon, famous aviator, do stunts in the air with his plane. Wenyon, who has had considerable experience in the air was with the Royal Air Forces in the late war and distinguished himself on several occasions. His capable handling of the plane was admired by the crowd who were there especially to see Mickey do his stunt.*

After enticing the crowd with several turns, dives and other aerial acrobatics, Wenyon leveled his plane, and Efferson prepared for his jump. Below, the eager crowd was transfixed as they waited for the daredevil to leave the plane. A short distance from the beach, a small Coast Guard boat stood ready to pluck the fearless Efferson, who claimed that he did not know how to swim, from the sea. According to the *Delaware Coast News*:

Rehoboth Survives the 1930s

About 4:45 the plane piloted by Wenyon circled high in the air over the Boardwalk and then due to the strong wind went inland about several hundred yards and then Mickey jumped. Soon the parachute opened and Efferson was floating gracefully through the air to land in the water of the Atlantic.

As the daredevil floated to earth, Wenyon circled the plane around the descending Efferson. The parachutist hit the water with a hard splash and disappeared beneath the surf. Efferson quickly freed himself from the parachute harness and, moments later, bobbed to the surface. The Coast Guard boat steamed over to Efferson and pulled the daredevil aboard. After Efferson was plucked from the ocean, he was brought ashore, where he was thronged by admiring youngsters. As he received a hero's welcome from the kids, a hat was passed so that spectators could contribute to a more substantial reward for the daring stunt. Efferson's jump was a bit more sedate than a modern sky diver's plunge, but the crowd was pleased. The daredevil was also satisfied with the amount collected when the hat was passed. He promised to return to Rehoboth Beach for a repeat performance.

Two years after Forrest Wenyon piloted the plane for Efferson's parachute jump at Rehoboth, Wenyon and John Beach Sr. established the Rehoboth Flying Club on the Dodd Farm, now the site of the Rehoboth Elementary School. Jack White had joined with his former teacher, Allie Buck, to form an aviation company known as Air Service, Inc. White served as the company's initial vice-president. Air Service, Inc. prospered for several years.

The end of the Roaring Twenties, the stock market crash and the onslaught of the Great Depression brought the heydays of the barnstorming aviators to an end. Financial strains forced Jack White to leave aviation and take up more economically stable pursuits. Interest in flying, however, continued to grow in Rehoboth. In 1938, the Rehoboth Airfield was officially opened. During the summer vacation season, flights were scheduled between College Park Airfield, outside Washington, D.C., and the resort. In addition, pilot instruction and sightseeing flights were offered at the Rehoboth Airport for several years. Eventually, however, the demands of modern aviation outpaced the airport's grass fields and other facilities. By the time that the Rehoboth Airport closed in 1986, barnstorming stunt pilots and Mickey Efferson, the boy who laughed at death, had become faded memories.

CELEBRATING THE FOURTH

Shortly after the Continental Congress adopted the Declaration of Independence in 1776, John Adams elatedly predicted that the anniversary of the break with Great Britain would be marked by grand celebrations. Adams wrote to his wife, Abigail:

> *I am apt to believe that it will be celebrated by succeeding generations as the great anniversary festival. It ought to be commemorated as the day of deliverance, by solemn acts of devotion to God Almighty. It ought to be solemnized with pomp and parade, with shows, games, sports, guns, bells, bonfires, and illuminations from one end of this continent to the other, from this time forward.*

When Rehoboth was established in 1873, Americans had been celebrating July Fourth for nearly a century, and in the early years of the resort, the town celebrated July Fourth with parades of carriages with bunting strewn through the spokes of their large wheels and filled with flag-waving riders. In the twentieth century, festivities became more active and included a five-and-a-half-mile race through the resort. In addition, the celebration moved to the beach. In 1928, the *Delaware Coast News* reported:

> *After the marathon, a very interesting program of sporting events were [held on] the beachfront. Races were participated in by the young, old, thin and fat and everyone seemed to enjoy the beach field meet.*

The races included a number of novelty events, such as pushing balloons across the sand, pie-eating, milk-drinking and other contests.

In 1930, July Fourth fell on a Friday, and on Thursday afternoon vacationers began to crowd into Rehoboth to celebrate the long holiday weekend. The *Delaware Coast News* reported:

> *On Thursday, July 3rd, practically every cottage within the corporate limits and in Dewey Beach were occupied by the owners or tenants. Friends and relatives all flocked to Rehoboth for visits over the holidays.*

As an endless stream of cars flooded into the resort throughout Thursday night and into Friday, an enterprising citizen noted the number of vehicles streaming across the bridge over the canal into Rehoboth on Independence Day. According to the *Delaware Coast News*:

Rehoboth Survives the 1930s

Patriotically decorated carriages parade through the resort on July Fourth. *Courtesy of the Delaware Public Archives.*

Rehoboth Beach

From Friday morning at 6 o'clock until that evening at 7 o'clock Mr. Theodore W. Palmer counted the cars crossing the bridge and stated that 3,911 cars came into Rehoboth and that each was packed with from four to seven people. Parking space in the resort was something that could not be had unless the car owners kept to the side streets and far down Rehoboth Avenue.

Not only were the hotels and rooming houses filled to capacity, but it also seemed that every private home was packed to overflowing with extra guests. Some holiday visitors abandoned any hope of finding solid accommodations, and they set up tents in Shaw Park near the canal at Rehoboth and Columbia Avenues. Shaw Park had been the original camp meeting grounds when Rehoboth was founded in 1873, but in 1930, motorists competed with the tents as they crammed their vehicles into every open lot in the park. The horde of holiday visitors invaded the stores, and the eager shoppers stripped the merchandise from the shelves. By the end of the weekend, the stores looked like deserted places of business with rows of empty racks.

It was reported that

the bathing beach was packed with bathers from the extreme end of the boardwalk at Dewey Beach to the section past Henlopen Avenue on the north...In front of Rehoboth Avenue, the beachfront was a mass of individuals together with fancy colored umbrellas, blankets, etc. during the afternoon of the Fourth, and again on Saturday and Sunday. The increased popularity of the bathing beach north of the Hotel Henlopen placed many bathers in this section. Here a beautiful scene was pictured with all kinds of descriptions of bathing attire, colored umbrellas, beach chairs, cots and tents.

Although a record-setting thirty thousand people were jammed into Rehoboth, it was a well-behaved crowd. The resort police force had been augmented by extra deputies, and they reported only a few minor traffic violations. In addition, the ocean was relatively calm, and the lifeguards had no problems with the thousands of people frolicking in the surf.

On the morning of July 4, a three-mile foot race was run through the streets of the resort, and some cars motored alongside the runners as they made their way through the town. Although the foot races, eating contests and other daytime activities seemed to be popular, they were overshadowed by the fireworks that were ignited at night. In 1930, Rehoboth remained faithful to John Adams's prediction that America's independence would be commemorated with a grand illumination. The *Delaware Coast Press* reported:

Rehoboth Survives the 1930s

During the evening a fire work display attracted a large crowd to the boardwalk and Frank L. Chase and his assistants had a fine collection of sparklers and sky rockets which illuminated the sky and which were enjoyed by the spectators.

THE RESORT IS WASHED AWAY

By the 1930s, veteran Rehoboth Beach residents were well aware of the damage a hurricane could do to their town. In the early days of the resort, some of the dunes had been leveled to make room for houses on the very edge of the beach, but after 1914, when a storm destroyed a line of cottages on Surf Avenue, many owners decided to move their buildings back from the dunes.

Oceanfront property continued to have a powerful allure, and in 1929, the Henlopen Hotel underwent a major renovation. According to the *Delaware Coast News*:

The rooms and corridors have been painted in a variety of warm harmonious tones, to correspond with the Spanish type of architecture of the building. Complete new bathroom fixtures and plumbing have been installed as well as an improved heating system. The rooms in the older section of the hotel will be refurnished throughout as well as some of the new section. New Public space and lobby furniture, draperies, etc., will be added and the kitchen equipment also entirely replaced to give the latest improved facilities in its food and service department.

In addition, a fifty-foot boardwalk with pavilion seats along its outer edge was constructed in front of the hotel. The first-story porches that once graced the Henlopen were converted into an enclosed solarium, and improvements were also made to the hotel's dance pavilion and dining room. Four small shops were added to the front of the building to serve customers using the boardwalk, and it was reported that "the result of these many improvements will give Rehoboth Beach a distinctive and modern hotel in every respect equal in beauty and appointments to those of larger Atlantic resorts."

As the resort grew, the natural tranquility of Rehoboth appeared secure, and the local newspaper commented:

Rehoboth's growth depends on the man and his family that is interested enough in the seashore to build his summer home and stay here during the

The refurbished Henlopen Hotel was a grand addition to the beachfront. *Courtesy of the Delaware Public Archives.*

Cars crowd around the portico to the Henlopen Hotel. *Courtesy of the Rehoboth Beach Historical Society.*

summer season. A large percentage of the cottage owners in the resort occupy their own cottages and this speaks well for the future of this Resort. The natural beauties of Rehoboth, the peace and quietude have a tendency to make this resort a family gathering place. The noise, hustle and bustle of the average ocean resort is missing from Rehoboth.

As the resort continued to develop, the memory of the 1914 storm seemed to fade, and for nearly two decades, owners of oceanfront property seemed safe—until August 1933.

The storm was born one thousand miles east of the West Indies, and it churned steadily across the warm waters of the Atlantic toward the United States. As the storm made its way up the Delmarva Peninsula, it drove massive waves onto the beaches. At Ocean City, Maryland, the torrential rain filled the coastal bay with water, while the hammering waves eroded the beach until the sand collapsed and the bay water rushed into the ocean. A new inlet had been created that severed the Maryland resort from Assateague Island.

Having permanently altered the Maryland coast, the hurricane continued northward into Delaware. After taking a swipe at Fenwick Island and Bethany Beach, the storm bore down on Rehoboth. In a repeat of what had happened in Ocean City, the waves ripped away at the beach and the rain began to accumulate in Silver Lake. According to the *Delaware Coast News*:

Silver Lake overflowed and the water coming in from the ocean flowed into the streets and flooded the cellars of the properties on Queen Street and Lakeside Drive. The piers belonging to Mrs. Watterman and Mr. Charles Watson were washed away. A group of firemen tried to cut an opening from the ocean to Silver Lake during the storm but after several attempts were unsuccessful.

A number of summer vacationers ventured down to the beach to get a glimpse of the awesome waves as they pounded the beach. Eventually, the ocean broached the dunes and flowed into town. According to the *Delaware Coast News*:

The Ocean waves, which assumed a height of from ten to fifteen feet broke consistently on the boardwalk. In the section [in front] *of the Hotel Henlopen, the waves broke over the boardwalk and the water raced down Lake Avenue a distance of several hundred yards. About five feet of the road at the intersection of Surf and Lake Avenue was undermined.*

While many residents of the coastal region took shelter as the storm hammered Rehoboth, there were those who took the opportunity to drive into the resort to see the towering waves. The *Delaware Coast News* reported that the resort was

> *regarded as a safe vantage point from which to view the unbridled forces of the raging seas. Hundreds of visitors, realizing with confidence its dependable safe conditions in this respect, journeyed to Rehoboth especially to view this tremendous spectacle.*

After the storm had passed, firemen returned to Silver Lake, where they were able to cut an opening across the dunes to the Atlantic. The excess water that accumulated in the lake gushed through the newly dug channel back into the ocean. Within a short time, the lake waters dropped to an acceptable level. As the waters receded from Rehoboth, the resort's residents quickly went to work to clean up the debris and return the town to normal.

According to the *New York Times*:

> *On the mainland hundreds of miles of paved roads, including up-to-date concrete highways, were under water, cracking up and otherwise dangerous for traffic. The famous Dupont Highway in Delware was closed from Dover, Del., to Salisbury, Md., where three bridges were swept like matchwood into destructive river currents. Everywhere telephone and telegraph wires snapped like so much knitting yarn.*

The paper went on to report:

> *Rehoboth Beach, Del., a fishing center and summer resort, was reported literally washed into the sea...Cape Henlopen, between Rehoboth and Lewes, Del., was reported to have been wiped out by the storm.*

After reading this grossly erroneous story, Wilbur Corkran, the developer of Henlopen Acres and one of the town's staunchest supporters, dashed off a letter to the editor of the *Times* that began: "I understand that a recent issue of your paper mentioned Rehoboth Beach, Del., as being washed out to sea, or words to that effect." Corkran continued by pointing out that Rehoboth was one of the few resorts on the Atlantic seaboard that was not separated from the mainland by a coastal bay: "The town is founded entirely on high land and has no marsh land between it and the mainland." Having established that the topography of Rehoboth helped protect it from most storms, Corkran lambasted the New York newspaper for reporting that the Delaware town had been destroyed:

> *It was neither washed out to sea nor seriously damaged. The total damage probably amounted to less than $2,000, being confined entirely to a sixty-foot section of the boardwalk being slightly unseated and few sections of railing being broken, principally benches being blown over against the railing. All of this damage was repaired within twenty-four hours after the storm.*

Corkran also pointed out that at the height of the storm, he and others had traveled around town to see the waves and monitor the damage. Corkran wrote to the *Times*:

> *With others I visited every part of Rehoboth Beach two or three times the day the storm was at its height and did not find a single building structurally damaged or people in a panicky condition. On the contrary, most of the residents, summer and otherwise, enjoyed the storm to the fullest extent and crowded down to the sea front to see the waves dash onto the beach.*

Hotel guests relax in the Henlopen's new solarium. *Courtesy of the Rehoboth Beach Historical Society.*

As Rehoboth was the "Nation's Summer Capital," Corkran reminded the editors of the *New York Times* that if they doubted the truth of what he had written, his "statements [could] be substantiated by judges, diplomats and other prominent people, not only from Washington's official life but of prominence from other States."

Over the years, Rehoboth has endured a number of violent storms. Some of these hurricanes had inflicted serious damage on oceanfront communities in neighboring states, but as Wilbur Corkran maintained, it would take more than a passing storm to wash Rehoboth into the sea.

DEATH TO MOSQUITOES

Mrs. Mary Wilson Thompson was in search of an army. She was, after all, the daughter of Major General James Harrison Wilson, who fought during the Civil War. General Wilson was an excellent organizer and a daring leader who commanded Union cavalry forces that helped win the war for the North. Sussex County historian Richard Carter wrote of Mary Thompson:

> *She was a person of almost ferocious competence and skill. Had she lived in a slightly later age, she could easily have won election to high political office (had she wished to pursue it). Yet she refused to consider that women should be made the political equals of men. She was a paradox of the passing of the Victorian era from Delaware.*

Thompson began visiting Rehoboth before World War I, and in the 1920s, she built a home in Rehoboth Beach, where she expected to spend long, relaxing summer days. But she had not reckoned on the swarms of insects that invaded the resort each year. Thompson recalled in her memoirs:

> *The only blot on the horizon seemed to be the mosquito question. When I first began to plant my garden, I did so with newspapers wrapped around my ankles, gloves on and a scarf wrapped around my neck. The situation was intolerable, and I was often forced to take refuge behind the screens.*

Thompson, however, was not about to back down from the irritating insects—she declared war. After she learned from a visitor that mosquitoes had been defeated in Panama by destroying the places where the insects live and breed, the general's daughter sprang into action.

Rehoboth Survives the 1930s

For generations, trash had been allowed to accumulate on the dunes, and this provided a convenient home for mosquitoes. Recruiting an army of mosquito killers, Thompson led an assault on the beach. Her troops carted away numerous truckloads of debris. As they dug through the rubbish, several old cars were found amid the trash.

As Thompson's forces got the upper hand on land, they launched an attack on the mosquitoes in the marshes. The swamp areas around the resort were cleared of rotting leaves and trees, and fish were added to the ponds to help control the insect population. After several years of work, a statewide survey indicated that Rehoboth Beach had fewer mosquitoes than any other Delaware town its size. Mary Thompson had the mosquitoes on the run, but the war was not over.

By now she was known as "the Mosquito Woman," but Thompson was not about to let the sneers of some of the residents of Rehoboth deter her. She had achieved a victory over the mosquitoes in the resort, but she knew that an enormous number of the insects lived in the marshes that lined the coast. Until these marshes were cleared of the insects, none of the Delaware coastal communities would be safe.

While Thompson was battling the mosquitoes in Delaware, the United Sates was plunged into the Great Depression. After President Franklin Roosevelt called for the creation of the Civilian Conservation Corps (CCC) to provide employment and to reinvigorate America's natural resources, Thompson rushed to Washington to lobby for the creation of a CCC camp in southern Delaware. Just thirty-seven days after Roosevelt took the oath of office, the first enlistee was enrolled in the Civilian Conservation Corps. Several weeks later, work began on CCC Camp 1224 near Lewes, and Mary Thompson was ready to call the troops to do battle against the mosquitoes.

When Camp 1224 was completed and the men started work, Thompson reported: "We have today a corps of 600 men under government employ, who are doing their best to ditch and clean our shores of the big bad mosquito." Thompson also said that the CCC would replicate the work that she had done in Rehoboth: "After the marshes will come the towns, when the proper stops will be taken to fill holes, clean drains, open gutters, etc."

As a general's daughter, Thompson knew that a single victory did not necessarily mean a successful campaign. In 1934, Thompson said:

> But in spite of all this work, without the women of the state co-operating it will all be of no avail. A rain-gutter clogged with leaves, a pail of water or a barrel left standing uncovered, a bird-bath become stagnant, will hatch enough mosquitoes to make life miserable for all. Absolute cleanliness, daily attention,

Bathers enjoy a mosquito-free beach. *Courtesy of the Delaware Public Archives.*

and no relaxation in inspecting premises is the only way. Unless we can convince the women of the necessity of co-operation, all will have been in vain.

As the dreaded mosquitoes began to disappear from the coast, the leaders of Rehoboth began to dream of bigger things for the resort. The *Delaware Coast News* declared:

> *Delaware, many people believe, has an ideal site for a real American Riviera, within a few hours' driving distance from any point in the state. This is between Rehoboth Beach and Bethany Beach, where there is a brand new amiesite* [asphalt] *road skirting the ocean front for about 13 miles.*

After a flurry of highway construction sparked by the building of the Du Pont Highway in the 1920s, road building in and around Rehoboth had slowed. One of the last pieces in Delaware's road network was a highway that would run down the coast from Rehoboth to Fenwick Island. After a number of false starts and delays caused by the Great Depression, survey work began on the portion of the coastal highway that connected Rehoboth with Bethany Beach in 1932.

Rehoboth Survives the 1930s

Only hardy motorists dared to drive across the sand from Rehoboth to Bethany Beach. *Courtesy of the Delaware Public Archives.*

The opening of the ocean road from Rehoboth to Bethany promised to be a boon for Rehoboth, which was expected to draw a significant number of visitors from Millsboro, Frankford, Dagsboro, Selbyville, Millville and Ocean View. Before the new road opened, residents of these communities had to take a circuitous route around the western reaches of the coastal bays to reach Rehoboth.

The new growth in Rehoboth was foreseen as the beginning of the development of the "American Riviera":

> *The state owns many acres of land along this strip, which is said to be available at reasonable prices. The road is there. The ocean with the splendid beach is there. The bay is not far away. The mosquitoes are losing out, the C.C.C. officials tell us. The climate is even more ideal than in New Jersey, it is considered by many. The summer season is longer. It is a paradise both in the bay and the ocean for fishing and crabbing and there is splendid shooting.*

While the army planned war games, vacationers planned to swim in the surf. *Courtesy of the Delaware Public Archives.*

Mary Wilson Thompson's army had defeated the mosquitoes, sparked continued growth in Rehoboth and initiated dreams of an American Riviera. She had won a victory that would have made her father proud.

THE ARMY INVADES THE BEACH

The invasion was unlike anything ever seen at Rehoboth. Army headquarters was inundated with reports from Dover, Wilmington and Philadelphia that a flood of men, guns and equipment was being ferried ashore from transports that had anchored within sight of the beach. The invaders were determined to strike at the industrial heart of America, and only quick action by the defending forces could stop them.

In 1934, the entrance to Delaware Bay, which was nearly in sight of Rehoboth Beach, was vital to the defense of America. A sprawling industrial complex stretched along the Delaware River from Philadelphia to Wilmington that contained ammunition factories, oil refineries, shipyards and other important industries. An attack up the bay could destroy a significant portion of America's war-making capacity and threaten the highly populated Northeast.

Rehoboth Survives the 1930s

Enemy warships that attempted to steam up Delaware Bay would have to pass the heavy guns of Fort Saulsbury at Slaughter Beach near the mouth of the Mispillion River. There were no fortifications on the Delaware coast, and an attack that began with enemy landings near Rehoboth would enable an enemy force to march northward and overwhelm Fort Saulsbury from the landward side. The bay would then be open to enemy warships and the stage set for an assault on the industries that lined the Delaware River.

With the world situation deteriorating rapidly during the 1930s, the United States was faced with the prospect that it might be attacked, and in 1934, General Douglas MacArthur decided to test the army's preparedness to meet an invasion along the Delaware coast. MacArthur's simulated attack extended across both sides of the bay and included landings in Delaware and New Jersey.

In the simulation, the attacking force was known as the "Black" army and the American defenders dubbed the "Blue" army. According to a report by the *New York Times* of MacArthur's exercise:

> *The "invading forces" of the Black entente which was landed on the New Jersey and Delaware coasts Monday were reported to be pushing slowly inland last night, their progress opposed only by scattered Blue patrols. The imaginary enemy, conjured up in military minds for the purpose of the army's "paper war," was reported to be slowly thrusting the spearhead of its advances toward the heart of the nation.*

As the imaginary invaders moved inland, the Blue army launched reconnaissance airplanes that "reported that the 'enemy' had established beachhead for the protection of its landings at Atlantic City, Port Norris and Cape May in New Jersey and at Rehoboth Beach in Delaware." In addition, scattered enemy patrols were pushing cautiously inland, and there were reports of skirmishes between small units of the Black and Blue forces. Major actions were not expected until the enemy had landed sufficient forces to make a successful stab toward Philadelphia.

In the simulation, towns in southern Delaware were evacuated, and available army units were rushed forward to fight delaying actions against invaders. The climactic encounter between the Blue and Black armies would not occur until the invaders had landed the bulk of their troops and the defenders had mobilized units in the Delaware and New Jersey areas.

According to the *New York Times*, "The imaginary war [was] soldierless, shotless, bloodless and entirely on maps, in minds and on paper." The newspaper went on to comment:

Whether or not the forces of the Black coalition, which has taken advantage of our preoccupation with another war in the Pacific to invade us, win or lose in the "paper war" must be decided by the army's umpires, also on paper.

While the invasion of Rehoboth by the phantom Black army failed to stir the resort, another government team descended on the coast in an attempt to bring long-term change to the area. In 1935, President Roosevelt established the Works Progress Administration (WPA) to build roads, construct public buildings and establish other programs to improve the economy.

The WPA created the Federal Writers' Project to compile and publish a travel guide for each state as a way of providing work for unemployed white-collar workers and to promote travel and tourism. *Delaware: A Guide to the First State* was published in 1938, and it described Rehoboth Beach as

one of the few spots along the South Atlantic coast where the mainland extends to the surf itself. Large stands of tall loblolly pine and holly, in the pines section of town, approach within a city block of the sea, forming an effective background to a widespread town of many small cottages, a few elaborate ones, and typical resort hotels and boarding houses.

The guide took due notice of the seasonal weekly rhythm of life in the resort:

In summer, during the early part of the week, Rehoboth has the appearance of a quiet residential community. Then at the week-end, visitors arriving by automobile, bus, and airplane tax the accommodations in the town, and holiday crowds sometimes cause an overflow into farmhouses within a 10-mile radius.

CHAPTER 6

ENEMY OFF THE COAST

WORLD WAR II DIMS THE TOWN

In 1941, the week after Thanksgiving marked the beginning of the Christmas shopping season, but on December 7, coastal residents did not go shopping. It was Sunday and all the stores were closed. After church, families spent the day quietly. Some gathered in the living room to listen to the professional football game between the Dodgers and the Giants; others listened to the music of Sammy Kaye. As they listened, the broadcasts were interrupted by the news that the Japanese had attacked the American fleet at Pearl Harbor, Hawaii.

When the Cape Henlopen Lighthouse toppled in 1926, the light of the great beacon was gone, but the coast did not go dark. The homes in Rehoboth boasted enough electric lights that, if combined, could send a signal to sea that would rival that of the collapsed lighthouse. On December 7, 1941, however, the bright lights of Rehoboth became a subject of great concern. The light from coastal communities silhouetted ships sailing past Rehoboth and made them easy targets for German submarines that were lurking off the coast.

Winter nights have always been dark along the Delaware coast, but none was blacker than the night of January 28, 1942, when German submarines prowled the waters off Rehoboth Beach. After the sun went down on January 28, Rehoboth held its first major blackout exercise. On that cold and snowy evening, representatives of the police and fire departments were joined by newly appointed air raid wardens to observe how coastal residents responded to the blackout. At 7:00 p.m., all vehicular traffic in Rehoboth Beach, Henlopen Acres and westward to Midway came to a halt. The cars and trucks sat motionless with their headlights extinguished. Around the stationary vehicles, all lights from nearby homes were put out. According to one report, had an enemy aircraft been flying over that part of the Delaware coast:

REHOBOTH BEACH

They would have looked down on a countryside in which the only light came from the whiteness of the snow which had fallen early in the evening, and which gave a ghostlike appearance to the streets that were devoid of all signs of normal life. They would not have known it, but down below them would have been a population of hundreds of people, ready to meet any emergency and not in the least afraid.

After three minutes, the test came to an end, and most members of the civil defense agencies considered the exercise a success. Except for a cottage on the south side of Silver Lake, which kept all lights burning through the entire three minutes of the drill, most coastal residents complied with the blackout regulations. One overzealous resident even extinguished the fire in her fireplace because she believed that an enemy pilot could see the glow as he flew overhead and looked down her chimney. There was, however, one unexpected source of light. At that time, radios were major pieces of furniture, and many featured large illuminated dials. The air raid wardens discovered that the lights from large radio dials were bright enough to be seen from a great distance.

In order to alert citizens of an impending air raid, Rehoboth Beach purchased a new alarm that was installed on the roof of city hall. According to a member of the town's civilian defense committee, the new alarm produced an inharmonious sound, and "it will wake all sleepers within a distance of two miles."

To alert residents that enemy aircraft were approaching, the Rehoboth alarm would sound three short blasts that were separated by ten-second intervals. The alert sequence would be sounded four times. If planes arrived overhead, the siren would sound a continual blast. On the other hand, two short blasts separated by fifteen-second intervals was the signal that the danger was over.

Coastal residents were advised to prepare for an attack by knowing their air raid warden, preparing a safe room in their houses, obeying the blackout regulations and having water and sand available to fight fires caused by incendiary bombs. In addition, residents were admonished to always carry a gas mask while walking or riding.

If a raid materialized, residents were to turn off all running water, gas and electricity before seeking shelter. If driving, coastal residents were advised to stop immediately, park the car and seek shelter. If they were riding or driving a horse, it should be unhitched from the vehicle and tied to a post by the halter lead.

After an air raid, coastal residents were not to leave their shelter until the all clear had been sounded on the town siren. In addition, the air raid

Enemy Off the Coast

WDC-Form No. 1
July 1942

No. ......6-13- 111..........................

War Damage Corporation

(A corporation created by Reconstruction Finance Corporation pursuant to Section 5d of the
Reconstruction Finance Corporation Act, as amended, herein called the "Corporation")

WASHINGTON, D. C.

1 ISSUED TO: .... ELLISON M. MEGEE ....
(herein called the "Insured")

2 Mail address: .... 203 BAYARD AVENUE, REHOBOTH BEACH, DELAWARE
....

3 Effective date: .... July 1st, 1942 ....

4   **In Consideration** of the payment of the premium, the Corporation agrees to indemnify the Insured, and
5 legal representatives, against direct physical loss of or damage to the property described in the attached application
6 which may result from **ENEMY ATTACK INCLUDING ANY ACTION TAKEN BY THE MILITARY, NAVAL**
7 **OR AIR FORCES OF THE UNITED STATES IN RESISTING ENEMY ATTACK.**
8   This insurance shall take effect on the effective date herein stated, at noon, standard time, at the place
9 where the property is located, and shall terminate twelve months thereafter, at the same hour.
10   The representations, terms and conditions of the application attached hereto shall be a part of this policy, and,
11 except as otherwise herein provided, this policy shall cover the property described in the application, for the amounts
12 therein stated, while located at the place(s) stated in the application, but not elsewhere.
13   Assignment of this policy shall not be valid except with the written consent of the Corporation.
14   The provisions printed on the following pages are made a part of this policy, and this policy shall also be
15 subject to such other provisions, stipulations and agreements as may be added hereto, over the signature of a duly
16 authorized Fiduciary Agent.
17   **In Witness Whereof,** the Corporation has executed this policy, but this policy shall not be valid unless
18 countersigned by a duly authorized Fiduciary Agent of the Corporation.

19   WAR DAMAGE CORPORATION

Attest:

A. T. Hobson
Secretary

W. L. Clayton
President

20 Countersigned this ......1st...... day of ......July............., 19..42

21 ....The Franklin Fire Insurance Co...
(Authorized Fiduciary Agent)

22   By...

With submarines off the coast, Rehoboth residents took out insurance against war damage.
Courtesy of the Rehoboth Beach Historical Society.

wardens carried a hand bell that also was used to indicate that the attack was over. When the danger had passed, residents were to check pilot lights to prevent a gas explosion. In addition, people were directed to remain at home and "avoid interfering by standing about in crowds in order to satisfy your curiosity."

The blackout regulations did little to allay fears that enemy agents could slip ashore on one of Delaware's dark beaches. Anyone who braved the dark night for a drive along the new coastal road to Bethany Beach needed to heed the Coast Guard's warning not to stop for any reason, even if they had a flat tire.

With the realization that their town might be attacked by enemy marauders, some residents of Rehoboth took out policies to insure their homes from war-related damage. Issued by the War Damage Corporation, the policies indemnified the Rehoboth homeowners from damage due to "enemy attack including any action taken by the military, naval, or air forces of the United States in resisting enemy attack." These insurance policies gave resort residents small comfort as they endured many dark nights and the occasional wail of the air raid siren.

HUNTING SUBMARINES ALONG THE COAST

In June 1942, vacationers arrived for the first wartime summer at Rehoboth and discovered the resorts dimmed by blackout regulations, armed patrols along the sand and the Delaware wing of the Civil Air Patrol (CAP) in the sky. With the American entry into the war, German U-boats began to appear in Delaware waters, and on February 2, 1942, the tanker *W.L. Steed* was torpedoed about one hundred miles from the coast. Two days later, German submarines sank the freighter *San Gil* and the tanker *Indian Arrow*. On February 28, two enemy torpedoes hit the destroyer *Jacob Jones*, and it sank in less than an hour. Five days later, the first CAP patrol flight took off from the Rehoboth base, which was constructed with donated lumber at Rehoboth Airport. Aircraft with a pilot and copilot flew cover over ship convoys as they steamed past the Delaware coast. When a suspicious vessel was sighted, the location was reported to the Army Air Corps in Dover, and a B-25 would be dispatched to bomb the sub.

On March 10, the Rehoboth CAP spotted its first enemy submarine as the U-boat was preparing to attack several vessels near the mouth of Delaware Bay. Pilots Eddie Edwards and Howard Carter dived their unarmed patrol plane toward the submarine, which immediately dived beneath the surface.

Enemy Off the Coast

Edwards and Carter circled their plane over the area for an hour, but the U-boat had steamed, submerged, to safer waters.

The flights of the Civil Air Patrol, the institution of the convoy system for ships and other measures drove most of the enemy submarines from the waters near Rehoboth. On December 23, 1942, John W. Chew Jr. flew over Rehoboth Beach with Howard Carter aboard as an observer. Chew and Carter were not looking for enemy subs. On this particular flight, they were testing signal flares.

As the CAP plane flew along the coast, Chew and Carter methodically dropped the flares and watched as the fiery signals descended to the water. Without warning, their plane also began to drop, and a few moments later it crashed into the chilly water one hundred yards from the beach.

On the beach, four Sea Scouts—William Massey, William Hamilton, Keith Coddington and Frank Small—saw the aircraft plunge into the waves, and they reacted instantly. Although it was December, they ran toward the wreckage, which remained partially afloat. Chew and Carter were alive in the aircraft, but the men were stunned, injured and swamped by the icy water.

As the four Sea Scouts ran across the sand, a crowd of spectators gathered to watch as the two pilots struggled to free themselves from the damaged plane. Without hesitation, the four teenagers pushed their way through the spectators, shed their clothes and sprinted toward the surf. Swimming through the rolling waves, the scouts reached the plane and pulled the two pilots from the wreckage. Neither Chew nor Carter was in much condition to swim, but the four teenagers were able to ferry the two pilots ashore.

Both pilots were taken to Beebe Hospital, where they spent several weeks recovering from the accident. The four Sea Scouts were taken first to the Maryland Avenue home of Mrs. Howard Sullivan. After they had been warmed up from their plunge into the freezing surf, they were transported to Beebe Hospital for examination. All except Small were discharged immediately after they were examined. Small was discovered to have a cold, and he was retained for a short time.

In March 1943, three months after the plane crash, Massey, Hamilton, Coddington and Small were honored for their heroic actions at a Civil Air Patrol ceremony held at the Rehoboth Airport. With members of the Rehoboth Beach Sea Scout Patrol in attendance, Major Hugh R. Sharp led the entire CAP corps in thanking the four teenagers. He said, "We invited you out here to do honor to four of your group. Their quick thinking and quick action saved our men. This base and the CAP as a whole appreciate what you have done for us." The four Sea Scouts also received individual letters of commendation from Major Earl Johnson. The national CAP commander called their lifesaving effort an "action of true bravery." He added, "I cannot find words to praise you enough, and your community should be proud of you."

CAVALRY TO THE RESCUE

Although the efforts of the Civil Air Patrol and others greatly reduced the number of submarine attacks in American waters, a new threat arose along the coast. In June 1942, two small bands of enemy agents landed on beaches near Jacksonville, Florida, and Amagansett, Long Island. The men carried maps and plans for a two-year program designed to destroy American war plants, railways, waterworks and bridges. All eight saboteurs were quickly arrested, but the fact that two groups of enemy agents had been able to reach shore unchallenged revealed a glaring vulnerability in America's coastal defense system.

After the capture of the enemy agents in Florida and New York, the Coast Guard began routine patrols of the nation's beaches. In Delaware, the soft sand made foot patrols difficult and ineffective, and the Coast Guard decided that the patrols would be able to see better and cover more of the beach if they were mounted on horseback

In 1943, a Coast Guard Mounted Patrol moved into stables at Rehoboth, and the newly recruited riders got their first taste of patrolling the Delaware beaches. Among the coast guardsmen on horseback were steeplechase riders and fox hunters from Philadelphia's Main Line, farm boys from the Midwest and cowboys from Texas. All of these coast guardsmen knew how to ride, which was gratifying to Captain W.L. McKinney, a twenty-nine-year-old cavalryman from the remount section of the Front Royal, Virginia Quartermaster Corps, who had been dispatched to Rehoboth to train the Coast Guard's new troopers.

McKinney taught the "Mounties" to gallop over the dunes, trot along the edge of the surf, dismount and, with every fourth man holding the horses, perform small arms drills. After two weeks of training, the Coast Guard's first cavalrymen were riding the wild beaches of Delaware.

Like their predecessors in the Life-Saving Service, the mounted coast guardsmen patrolled only at night or when bad weather during the day reduced visibility. Just as the surfmen of the Life-Saving Service had done a generation earlier, when the coast was hit by a storm, the patrols went on around the clock as the Mounties rode through snow, sleet and rain to ensure that no enemy saboteur landed on the Delaware coast.

After each four-hour patrol, the men would spend an hour or so rubbing down their horses. In addition, the men had to clean and dry the saddles and bridles. In the tradition of the old-time cavalry, the horses were treated with baby-like care. Each animal had its own formula of oats, corn, bran and hay that was written on a slate board over its stall.

In addition to their splendid horses, the uniforms issued to the Mounted Patrol made the Coast Guard unit one of the snappiest-looking outfits in the armed services. Although they wore the standard sailors' pea jacket, the Mounties were outfitted with blue riding breeches and brown field boots. The uniform was topped off with a hard-weather cap. The serious nature of the work done by the Coast Guard Mounted Patrol was reinforced by the ammunition belt worn around the rider's waist and the rifle slung in a holster on the horse's right side. The uniform was as practical as it was attractive. "It's got to be that way," the veteran cavalryman McKinney once remarked. "These men are going to be the hardest-working men in the Coast Guard just as the cavalry was always the hardest working branch of the army."

In February 1943, Captain E.A. Coffin (captain of the Port of Philadelphia and commandant of the Coast Guard for the Fourth Naval District) arrived to inspect the Mounted Patrol, and McKinney put his new troopers through their paces. After a look at the Coast Guard Mounties wheeling through cavalry maneuvers with the skill of tough old horse troopers, Coffin announced:

> It is already clear that the Mounted Patrol will be enormously helpful in protecting our shoreline against all kinds of enemy activity. The patrol has proven its value in actual work on the beaches, and we are ready now to extend it rapidly.

For the rest of the war, the Coast Guard mounted patrolmen methodically made their way along the Delaware dunes as they scanned the seacoast frontier for any sign of hostile vessels.

SHIP ASHORE

Perhaps it was the February weather that caused the misguided whale to lose its bearings. Maybe it was the unusual ship traffic caused by World War II. Possibly the whale just got lost. In 1944, the huge creature swam into the Roosevelt Inlet, worked its way past the center of Lewes and headed down the canal toward Rehoboth. The *New York Times* reported:

Residents of this area wondered today whether that whale they saw swimming peacefully down the Lewes-Rehoboth Canal ever got back to the ocean. The whale came into the canal on an exceptionally high tide, whipped by stiff winds, and when first sighted was only two miles from the ocean. But it was a fifteen-mile swim the way it was headed, for it would have to pass through Rehoboth and Indian River bays and out Indian River inlet.

The rare appearance of the whale in the canal enabled Rehoboth residents to turn away from the grim news of the war, but in September the resort could not ignore a more common adversary. Early in the month, a hurricane was born in the warm waters of the Atlantic, and by September 12, the storm was packing winds over 130 miles per hour as it thrashed its way past the Florida coast. After the eye of the stormed nipped Cape Hatteras, the hurricane ran northward off the coast of the Delmarva Peninsula. Although the center of the storm was 50 miles from the beach, gusts estimated at 150 miles per hour lashed the shore. The storm flooded Fenwick Island and cut the Bethany Beach boardwalk to pieces. The high wind and water of the hurricane flooded across the dunes, inundated Route 1, uprooted trees, destroyed utility poles, ripped boats from their moorings and sank a barge in the Lewes and Rehoboth Canal.

With the storm lashing the coast, the captain of the 254-foot-long tanker *Thomas Tracy* decided to seek shelter behind the Delaware Breakwater. As the ship neared Cape Henlopen, the tanker was struck by the powerful northeast winds of the approaching hurricane. Under normal circumstances, the engines of the *Thomas Tracy* would drive the tanker into Delaware Bay and safety, but the tanker's engines failed. The winds were so strong that the tanker was pushed southward past the high dunes of Cape Henlopen, past Peter Marsh's old house and past the Henlopen Hotel to near the center of Rehoboth Beach. By now, the vessel was perilously close to the shore.

The hurricane drove the disabled tanker onto the sand, and the ship came to rest at the foot of Brooklyn Avenue. With the forward section of the *Thomas Tracy* firmly grounded on the beach, the stern portion of the vessel was pounded by the breakers. It was not long before the loud cracking sound of splitting metal announced that the ship's steel back had been broken. The broken hull of the *Thomas Tracy*, with a telltale crack running up its side, settled into the sands of Rehoboth Beach.

The storm continued northward, where it plowed its way across eastern Long Island, Rhode Island and Massachusetts. In its wake, what became known as the Great Atlantic Hurricane had sunk five ships, killed 390 people

The *Thomas Tracy* sits across the beach from a damaged boardwalk. *Courtesy of the Rehoboth Historical Beach Society.*

and caused $100 million in damages in the United States. In Delaware, the Rehoboth Beach boardwalk had been severely damaged, trees were uprooted and power was out throughout the coastal region.

According to the *Delaware Coast News*:

> *Linemen of the Electric Company worked furiously to clear the streets of fallen trees. Food deterioration in refrigerators has been a problem of home owners and restaurants. The U.S. Army lent timely help in clearing the Pines sections of the resort, working til 4 o'clock Friday morning, and again back on the job that afternoon. The Army crews were volunteer members of the amphibious duck detachment stationed at Deauville Beach. They used army motorized derricks in hauling off huge fallen trees around Columbia and Henlopen Avenue, that caused much of the damage to electric wires in the Pines.*

As the downed trees were removed and the power lines repaired, people began to return to the streets of Rehoboth. According to the *Delaware Coast News*:

> *A steady stream of cars poured into Rehoboth Beach over the week end to see the huge hull of the wrecked tanker,* Thomas Tracy, *lying on the beach,*

Waves batter the *Thomas Tracy*. *Courtesy of the Delaware Public Archives.*

Curious residents get a close-up look at the beached *Thomas Tracy. Courtesy of the Rehoboth Beach Historical Society.*

and other damages here and at Lewes from the 75 mile an hour hurricane last Thursday. To see the bathing suit crowd back on the sunny beach [the] next day, sporting in a calm surf, it would never be suspected that twenty-four hours earlier the same surf was a black, mountainous wall of destruction. Several thousand visitors jammed the resort over the weekend.

The *Thomas Tracy* had grounded over the wreckage of the *Merrimac*, which had been driven onto the beach in 1918. Salvagers soon arrived to cut the *Thomas Tracy* to pieces so that the tanker could be carted away. Chunks of the lower part of the ship were too difficult to salvage, and these were left behind. Occasionally during very low tides, the steel scraps from the *Thomas Tracy* can be seen mingled with the wooden timbers of the *Merrimac* as a vivid reminder of the fury of the Great Atlantic Hurricane.

PEACE AT LAST

During the first week of May 1945, the low rumbles of the booming guns at Fort Miles mingled with the joyous sound of church bells as the people of Rehoboth learned that Germany had surrendered. According to the *Delaware Coast News*, on Tuesday, May 8, 1945:

Enemy Off the Coast

The wheels of industry around the Delaware Capes paused en mass Tuesday, following President Harry Truman's proclamation at 9 a.m. of victory in Europe. Simultaneously with the blasting of radios emanating from practically every home in the two towns of Rehoboth Beach and Lewes, church bells began to ring and continued for a period of 30 minutes.

As the *Delaware Coast News* noted:

The European phase of World War II came to an end at 8:41 p.m. Eastern War Time on Sunday, May 6th...Everywhere throughout the nation doors of churches were open to receive worshippers, with any unable to reach the church of their choice, praying where they stood. A feeling of reverence seemed to greet the news of Germany's surrender. Many in the throngs were heard to say, "The battle is only half won."

Following the defeat of Germany, the dropping of atomic bombs on Hiroshima and Nagasaki gave the United States an edge that would bring the war to a speedy end. On August 17, 1945, the *Delaware Coast News* was finally able to report: "On Tuesday night the world heard of the glad tidings of Victory over Japan."

The news of victory over Japan touched off the most tumultuous demonstration ever witnessed on the coast:

When the radio flashed the electrifying news at 7 o'clock after a long day of waiting and impatience at the uncertain bulletins, Rehoboth and Lewes residents were suddenly galvanized into action. Nervous tensions of the past few days suddenly snapped into one tremendous uproar. Those who had not heard the radio flash were first aware of Victory by the blare of the old Rehoboth Air-raid siren. The Fire Company sirens in both towns entered the din.

While the Rehoboth fire siren blasted away for two solid hours, the fire company rolled every piece of its equipment onto the streets, including an old obsolete engine. With kids climbing aboard the engines, the fire company led a parade through the streets of the resort that lasted for several hours. The blare of the fire siren was barely audible over the sounds of screaming car horns. The parade was joined by a car trailing a huge bell, whose repeated gongs added to the general cacophony. At the corner of First Street and Rehoboth Avenue, a little girl sat on the curb and mechanically beat on a frying pan with a kitchen spoon.

Although the United States was at war, Rehoboth was still filled with vacationers, and many visitors at the resort were eating dinner when the news arrived:

> *Diners in restaurants forgot all about their food. Many left filled plates and got out on the street. At the Dinner Bell Inn, when the first newscaster had completed the announcement and the National Anthem was played, people rose spontaneously to their feet and stood in silence. Tears were in many eyes when they sat down.*

The victory over Germany and Japan ended World War II, but the people of the Delaware coast were well aware that peace had come at a great price. As the *Delaware Coast News* noted, there were some who did not join in the celebration at Rehoboth:

> *And there must have been many tears behind closed doors. There were some who could not join the glad parade. Their sons who had helped to give peace to the world will never come home again. We who rejoice salute those brave souls whose loved ones made the Supreme Sacrifice.*

CHAPTER 7

THE RESORT BLOSSOMS

REHOBOTH GOES TO SEA

The eager crowd that gathered at Rehoboth Beach City Hall did not think of Joshua Fisher as they waited for the buses to arrive. The caravan of cars and buses that assembled on January 3, 1949, was scheduled to leave at 11:30 a.m., and latecomers were to be left behind. The convoy was bound for Philadelphia and the ceremonies aboard the USS *Rehoboth*. On that January morning, Joshua Fisher was far from the minds of the people of the resort, but he should have been in the forefront.

In 1756, Fisher utilized the experience of Lewes pilots, his own knowledge of the bay and the available scientific measurements to produce the first comprehensive chart of the bay. According to the eminent coastal historian Hazel Brittingham, Joshua Fisher's map of the Delaware Bay "retained its usefulness as a guide until the publication of a comprehensive chart by the U.S. Coast Survey almost a century later."

Fisher's chart was an important contribution to the knowledge of coastal waters, and in 1949, there were still areas of the Seven Seas that were yet to be mapped. The people in the caravan of cars that left Rehoboth for Philadelphia were eager to see that work continued with the recommissioning of the USS *Rehoboth*. The *Rehoboth* had been built during World War II as a seaplane tender, and in 1948 it was refitted as a hydrographic survey ship. The three-hundred-foot vessel was equipped with a small laboratory and an array of scientific instruments. Continuing the tradition that Joshua Fisher established in Delaware, the *Rehoboth* sailed to uncharted corners of the seas to retrieve specimens of the ocean bottom, measure ocean temperature and take samples of seawater at different depths.

On the day of the recommissioning ceremonies, the buses at Rehoboth Beach were quickly loaded, and the caravan headed out of town. After the

Above: The USS *Rehoboth* charted the depths of the Pacific Ocean. *Courtesy of Bob De Blasi.*

Left: A crewman aboard the USS *Rehoboth* prepares to make a measurement. *Courtesy of Bob De Blasi.*

cars and buses reached the Philadelphia Navy Yard, the dignitaries filed aboard the ship. During the ceremonies, the delegation from Rehoboth presented the ship's crew a silver service that included a large tray, coffeepots and teapots, a cream pitcher and a sugar bowl. In addition, the ship was presented with a radio record player and twenty-eight albums of classical and popular music.

During the next two decades, the *Rehoboth* took careful measurements of the wind, water and ocean currents. The vessel was affectionately known as the "Rebop" by its crew of more than 150 men, some of whom considered assignment to the survey vessel tough duty for a peacetime ship. Cruises aboard the *Rehoboth* sometimes lasted as long as nine months. During these extended voyages, the ship spent up to thirty days at sea before putting into port for fuel and provisions. The *Rehoboth* stopped at Midway, Pearl Harbor and Adak, Alaska, as the survey vessel crisscrossed the Pacific Ocean and the crew took scientific measurements to unlock some of the mysteries of the ocean.

To help break the monotony of shipboard life, the ship's cooks held regular barbecues on the vessel's afterdeck. Crewmen fashioned grills from discarded fifty-gallon drums, and charcoal was bought when the vessel was in port. The menu usually featured fresh pineapple, potato salad, baked beans, grilled steaks and soft drinks.

By the time that Bob De Blasi shipped aboard the *Rehoboth* in 1957, the ship had logged thousands of miles cruising the Pacific Ocean. Aboard the *Rehoboth*, De Blasi served as a second-class aerographer's mate and a weatherman, and he witnessed the *Rehoboth*'s most spectacular service. In 1958, the United States conducted a series of atomic tests at the Eniwetok and Bikini Atolls in the Marshall Islands. Years later, De Blasi recalled:

> *I witnessed the detonation of ten bombs…They were detonated from various distances and places—surface, barge, high altitude balloon, from 200 miles to 6 miles. We were part of a task group of many ships of assorted types.*

In particular, De Blasi recalled Shot Wahoo:

> *The detonation was on May 16, 1958 at 13:30 hours. The Navy wanted to find out the effects of an underwater atomic bomb on submarines… [On] the afternoon of the shot, Rehoboth was lying to about six miles from ground zero along with the rest of the task group…In the distance a huge plume of water rose up. Shortly, the primary shock wave hit the hull of the ship with a loud "bang!"*

The crew of the USS *Rehoboth* enjoys a barbeque on the afterdeck on July 4, 1958. *Courtesy of Bob De Blasi.*

After the secondary shock wave struck *Rehoboth*'s hull, the ship got underway, and the scientists began to track the radiation readings and plot. In addition, De Blasi and other crewmen took soundings and used trawling nets to collect marine life.

In addition to Shot Wahoo, the *Rehoboth* participated in other atomic tests. De Blasi recalled:

> *The other shots I witnessed usually went off between 0500–0600 hours. After breakfast, we would sit on deck on the opposite side of the shot with our hands over our eyes. Only the officers and the scientists had special goggles to look directly at the fireball. Again [there was] the countdown on the PA. Then a bright light would envelop the whole area…Immediately you would feel the heat emitted by the shot even though we may have been 8, 15, or 20 miles away. The shock waves could be felt as well. Over the years I have told people and students of this experience and of observing a nuclear cloud. It was spectacular! There it was, a rising, boiling cloud colored in hues of reds, oranges, and browns. If it were not so deadly, you would categorize it as something surreal and beautiful. When it hit about 45,000 or 50,000 feet, it spread out into the familiar mushroom shape and dropped radioactive fallout.*

The Resort Blossoms

De Blasi and the other sailors had no special shield from the fallout that rained down on the *Rehoboth*:

> *The only protection we had was our skin and the clothes we wore. We were issued a radiation badge upon entering the proving ground. However, this only measured the amount of gamma radiation received and not alpha, beta or other radiation. Were we concerned about our health? I was 21 years old and most of the crew was in the 20–30 year old category. You don't think of those things at that age. By the way, we were never told of the dangers of being exposed to radiation nor were we told of the radiation doses received.*

After participating in the atomic tests, the *Rehoboth* continued to help map the seas of the world until the vessel was decommissioned, and in 1970, the ship was scrapped. During its career, the *Rehoboth*'s oceanic research helped mariners better understand the dangers at sea so that they could navigate the oceans in safety. Joshua Fisher would have been proud.

A BRIDGE FAR, FAR AWAY

On July 30, 1952, a crowd estimated at twenty thousand people, plus Francis the Talking Mule, watched as a caravan of vehicles led by Maryland governor Theodore R. McKeldin started forward across the bridge. As they drove ahead, the dignitaries were marking the fulfillment of a decades-old dream that would dramatically change Rehoboth Beach.

Until the early 1950s, Rehoboth remained a tranquil coastal town whose residents were content with the way things were. The resort's collection of beach cottages, guesthouses and hotels was modest compared to major Atlantic resorts. According to the *New York Times*:

> *It is at Rehoboth that one meets for the first time the beautiful, wide, white, beach and rolling surf so typical of the whole coastline. Although Rehoboth is still essentially a summer cottage community—some of the cottages, particularly in the pine woods at the north end of town, are fairly luxurious—it does have the appurtenances of a typical resort, since its summer claims are the main* raison d'être.

Although Rehoboth had a permanent population of several thousand, and during a summer weekend, as many as fifty thousand visitors would crowd into the town, the Delaware resort lacked the hustle and bustle of some other major seashore destinations. The *Times* reported, "There is a mile-long boardwalk with a number of concessions and pick-up eating places. There are some public locker facilities, a great many boarding houses, and several good restaurants."

Despite its laid-back nature, signs that Rehoboth was undergoing pervasive changes began to appear on the beach. The old-style swimsuits had been replaced with more colorful, form-fitting swim attire that some found scandalous. Some visitors even wore shockingly brief two-piece "bikinis." In addition, the State of Maryland was putting the finishing touches on a mammoth construction project that would soon flood the beach at Rehoboth with thousands of new visitors.

After World War II, many vacationers from Washington and Baltimore were eager to drive to the Delaware coast, but they were faced with two unpleasant routes. They could drive north on Route 40 until they reached the head of the Chesapeake Bay and then head southeast across the Delmarva Peninsula to Rehoboth. Small towns, traffic lights and other obstacles along this route made this drive a challenge. On the other hand, vacationers could drive to Annapolis, where they would board a ferry for a trip across the bay. The wait for the ferry to arrive and load added as many as four hours to the trip, and for years, motorists yearned for a bridge across the bay.

After World War II, strollers on the boardwalk continued to stop at the WCTU fountain. *Courtesy of the Delaware Public Archives.*

The Resort Blossoms

In the early twentieth century, when the first cars were beginning to rumble into Rehoboth, the first serious plan to bridge the Chesapeake Bay was proposed and quickly died due to the excessive cost. After decades of debate, construction on the bridge finally began in 1949, and three years later, Governor McKeldin led the caravan of dignitaries in a leisurely drive across the bay.

When the Chesapeake Bay Bridge opened, the *New York Times* predicted:

> *Millions of sweltering residents of Baltimore and Washington will undoubtedly be tempted by the new bridge to explore the surf bathing possibilities that will now be only three or four hours driving time instead of the seven or eight hours because of the long waits for the ferry.*

It was thought that by 1961, 1.1 million vehicles would use the bridge each year, but within five years, nearly three times that many motorists were taking advantage of this quick and easy way of crossing the Chesapeake. Among those millions of drivers were thousands of summer vacationers headed for Rehoboth, which inevitably experienced a building boom similar to that of the 1920s.

REHOBOTH BATTLES THE SEA

By 1962, the opening of the Chesapeake Bay Bridge, improvements to roads across the Eastern Shore and economic prosperity sent thousands of visitors to Rehoboth Beach, where business owners expanded to accommodate the ever-growing number of vacationers. The resort was poised for a long period of steady growth, but the prospect for increased development came to a halt in March, when the barometer began to fall and storm clouds started to gather over the Delaware coast.

Over the centuries, the land between the head of Rehoboth Bay and Cape Henlopen had always been a target of ocean storms. During the late summer, tropical hurricanes were known to have visited the Rehoboth area, and during the rest of the year, slow-moving nor'easters pounded their way along the coast. Named for the northeasterly winds generated by counterclockwise low pressure systems at their core, these lumbering storms could hammer the coast for days.

The summer encampments of the Native Americans were usually abandoned when most of the severe storms swept the coast. In October 1693, there were only a few European colonists living near the head of Rehoboth Bay when a strong storm smashed the dunes, and the storm damage was quickly repaired. By the time that Peter Marsh had established the Homestead in the eighteenth century, more settlers had established themselves in the Rehoboth area, but they soon recovered from a hurricane that passed over Cape Henlopen in 1749.

During the first half of the nineteenth century, several hurricanes struck the Rehoboth region, but the lack of development at the beach kept damage to a minimum. The threat from ocean storms, however, was dramatically increased when the resort was established in 1873. For the first time, there was significant development within striking distance of any large storm. In 1914, a storm ripped up the boardwalk and washed Surf Avenue into the ocean. The damage was repaired, but four years later a storm drove the ships *Merrimac* and *Severn* onto the beach. The resort did sustain some damage during the 1933 storm, but as Wilbur Corkran clearly pointed out, "It was neither washed out to sea nor seriously damaged." The same could be said of the storm that had driven the *Thomas Tracy* ashore in 1944. Rehoboth may have been battered and bruised, but it survived nature's pounding pretty much intact. None of these storms, however, could match the brute strength of the nor'easter that arrived on Ash Wednesday 1962.

During the first week of March, the tides were unusually high when a high-pressure system over eastern Canada helped stall and combine two low-pressure systems off the Atlantic coast to create a nor'easter of epic proportions. As the slow-moving storm inched its way along the Delaware shore, Rehoboth was hit with gale-force winds, torrential rains and a series of devastating high tides. For several days, the wind and water of the lingering storm ripped into the resort. The boardwalk, homes, hotels and other structures began to give way and filled the resort's flooded streets with tons of debris.

During the height of the storm, some residents of Rehoboth hunkered down in their homes, whose windows and doors shook in the gale-force winds. Others retreated to the Rehoboth fire hall, where cots, sleeping bags and blankets littered the floor. Eventually, as the lumbering storm moved off the coast, the residents began to take stock of the damage. What they discovered was a swath of devastation unlike anything ever seen before along the coast. The day after the storm subsided, the *Delaware Coast Press* reported:

> *Disaster, without any forewarning, struck the Rehoboth Beach, Lewes and Dewey Beach area on Tuesday and Wednesday of this week, causing damage to properties estimated at over $10 million. The havoc was so great it belies the imagination...It was the worst flood and windstorm ever to strike this area. The devastation was terrible, especially at Rehoboth Beach where boardwalk, businesses places and homes were smashed, splintered and inundated by pile-driving 40-foot waves and powerful tides.*

Debris from the 1962 storm littered the streets of the resort. *Courtesy of the Delaware Public Archives.*

The storm lifted houses from their foundations. *Courtesy of the Delaware Public Archives.*

The newspaper went on to report:

Almost the entire boardwalk had been destroyed, washed out to sea. Even the new concrete block-long boardwalk section at the end of Rehoboth Avenue was torn apart by the pounding of the mountainous waves. Entire business places were beaten to splinters and completely disappeared, swallowed up by the roaring surf.

Among the major casualties was the Henlopen Hotel, which had a major portion of its front section wiped away by the storm. North of the resort, Henlopen Acres and North Shores were flooded, and south of town, the ocean highway from Dewey Beach to Fenwick Island was underwater.

As soon as the winds abated and the water receded, the coastal area was invaded by an estimated eight hundred members of the National Guard and fifty state troopers who worked with the region's fire departments, police departments, civil defense volunteers, Coast Guard and other service personnel

The 1962 stormed ripped the front off the Henlopen Hotel. *Courtesy of the Delaware Public Archives.*

to secure the devastated area and assist those affected by the storm. Streets were clogged with mounds of sand and piles of splintered buildings, broken furniture and other debris. With the opening of the vacation season only a few months away, it appeared that Rehoboth faced one of the most dismal years on record.

From March to Memorial Day, hordes of workers swarmed over Rehoboth to clean the streets, repair buildings and reconstruct the boardwalk. As the work of rebuilding went on, travel writers were invited to visit Rehoboth in May, and they were astonished by what they found. Instead of the devastated resort that had been pictured in numerous national publications, they found a seaside town with improved visitor accommodations, a rebuilt boardwalk and a new oceanfront look. There may have been some storm scars visible when the first vacationers arrived in June, but Rehoboth Beach was back in business!

THE RESORT TODAY

Francis Jordan initially visited Rehoboth before the Civil War, more than a decade before the resort was established. At that time, the only structure that he found in the area was a rough plank shed that had been built by sportsmen who hunted wildfowl during the fall shooting season. In 1879, however, Jordan noted, "Since then a veritable city by the sea has sprung up, almost in a night, and bids fair to outstrip many of its older and better known rivals."

Jordan was attracted to the beach by reports of Native American shell mounds, and he wanted to investigate an area that lay just beyond the burgeoning cottages, hotels and other structures that lined the beach. About five hundred feet from the beach, he discovered a hard ribbon of land that had been packed solid by the feet of Native Americans who had vacationed here long before the first European arrived on the coast.

Lining the band of tightly packed soil were several hundred small mounds that contained clam, oyster and mussel shells, together with pieces of charcoal. The small conical piles of shells and other debris had been left behind by the Native Americans when they vacationed at the beach. Over a century ago, Jordan commented, "So far as I have been able to ascertain, no similar example of an encampment possessing the same archaeological value exists on the Atlantic seaboard."

Jordan had discovered the strip of land that lay just beyond the new cottages of Rehoboth Beach that had once been the site of the summer Native American encampment, and he wrote:

REHOBOTH BEACH
MUSEUM

The Rehoboth Beach Museum stands as a guardian of the resort's past. *Courtesy of the Rehoboth Beach Historical Society.*

Hither for many centuries they annually came to escape the enervating heat of the inland villages, and probably remained far into the autumn, or until the geese and ducks, with which the bay and lakes are stocked at this period, deserted those placid waters for a warmer climate.

As important as this discovery was, he recognized that he lacked the resources to investigate further. In addition, he saw that the remains of Delaware's first ocean resort would soon be swallowed up by the growth of the coast's newest resort:

In conclusion, I have only to express the regret that I have not been permitted to make as thorough examination of the remains of this ancient Indian village as their value to archaeology certainly entitles them to. My regret is intensified because of the very near approach of that time when there will be no further opportunity for research. Even as I write embryo streets traverse its domain in every direction, and in the space of perhaps only a few months, lofty hotels and comfortable cottages will rise upon the site of the Indian wigwam, and every trace of the aboriginal character of the spot will have disappeared before the march of improvement.

In the years following Jordan's discovery, the resort, of course, continued to grow, and much of the archaeological evidence left by the Native Americans, the early colonists and other significant figures in the history of Rehoboth Beach has been lost. Following its recovery from the 1962 storm, Rehoboth continued to grow for the rest of the decade. During that time, many coastal areas were engulfed in a wave of condominium construction that left the dunes dotted with high-rise towers. At Rehoboth, height restrictions kept these modern intrusions to a minimum, and the resort began to sprawl its way over the canal and into the fields to the west.

The Resort Blossoms

In 1977, archaeologist Dan Griffith led a routine field survey team to investigate areas around Rehoboth Bay that lay in the path of future development. Combining documentary evidence with what he discovered on the ground, Griffith concluded that he had uncovered the location of Captain John Avery's homestead. At that time, no extensive archaeological work was done, but the site was listed on the National Register of Historic Places by the United States Department of the Interior.

For two decades, Avery's Rest lay undisturbed, but by 2007, development approached the site of the house of the captain-colonist. Griffith and other archaeologists began work to discover as much as possible about Avery's home. During digs in 2007 and 2008, they unearthed a number of colonial features, including a well that was lined with a square box frame. In addition, archaeologists discovered a number of pottery fragments, pipe stems and other artifacts associated with the seventeenth-century colonist.

In 2008, a large cellar hole was located that may have been part of Avery's house or a cellar to an outbuilding, such as a storehouse. The artifacts recovered include a Spanish silver coin, high-style ceramics and evidence of cattle and pig raising. Some documents indicate that Avery hired Native

Archaeologists relax in Captain John Avery's cellar. *Courtesy of the Archaeological Society of Delaware, Sussex County Chapter.*

The Rehoboth Beach Museum has become a repository for items from the resort's past. *Photo by Tom Morgan.*

Americans to hunt deer for him, and some Indian artifacts, deer bones and antlers were also unearthed.

Avery's Rest is one of few seventeenth-century rural farmsteads excavated by professional archaeologists in coastal Delaware, and the ongoing archaeological work in Rehoboth is adding significantly to a better understanding of the area's history. In addition, other groups have been hard at work preserving the resort's past. After the trains stopped running and the tracks were torn up, the railroad station suffered many years of neglect. In 1985, the nonprofit Rehoboth Railroad Preservation Society was formed to save and preserve this reminder of a time when trains were vital to the resort. The station was moved to Lighthouse Island Park on Rehoboth Avenue near the Lewes and Rehoboth Canal.

The Rehoboth Beach Historical Society was formed in 1974, and at its museum on Rehoboth Avenue near the canal, the society collects and displays artifacts, documents, photographs and other historically significant materials. The museum sits next to the restored railroad station used by the resort's chamber of commerce, and a short distance away, a large-scale model of the Cape Henlopen Lighthouse greets visitors entering the resort as a reminder of the richness of the resort's past.

BIBLIOGRAPHY

NEWSPAPERS

Baltimore Sun, October 5, 1952.

Delaware Beachcomber, July 12, 1996.

Delaware Coast News, May 19, June 12 and July 7, 1928; March 28 and April 20, 1929; November 28, 1930; May 15, 1931; December 9 and December 30, 1932; January 27, August 18 and August 25, 1933; January 1, 1934; August 2, 1935; December 12 and December 19, 1941; January 30, February 6 and May 15, 1942; January 1, February 12 and May 19, 1943; September 22, 1944; May 11 and August 17, 1945; and December 30, 1948.

Delaware Coast Press, March 5 and March 11, 1997; April 1, 1998; and February 2, 2002.

Milford Chronicle, April 20, 1917.

New York Times, August 8, 1914; August 24 and September 4, 1933; August 29, 1934; February 25, 1944; and August 3, 1952.

Rehoboth Beacon, July 1873.

Salisbury Times, March 14, 1942.

PERIODICALS

Benson, Barbara E. "Delaware Goes to War." *Delaware History* 24, no. 3–4 (Spring/Summer 1995; Fall/Winter 1995).

Cox, S.S. "The Life Saving Service." *The North American Review* (May 1881).

Doughty, Frances Albert. "Life at a Life-Saving Station." *Catholic World* 65, no. 388 (July 1897).

Gilmore, Jann Haynes. "Ethel Pennewill Brown Leach: Delaware Artist of Time, Place, and Season." *Delaware History* 28, no. 2–3 (1998–99).

Hancock, Harold B., ed."William Morgan's Autobiography and Diary: Life in Sussex County, 1780–1857." *Delaware History* 19, no. 1 (Spring/Summer 1980).

Higgins, Anthony, ed. "Mary Wilson Thompson Memoir." *Delaware History* 18, no. 1–3 (Spring/Summer 1978; Fall/Winter 1978; Spring/Summer 1979).

Merryman, James H. "The United States Life-Saving Service." *Scribner's Magazine* 19, no. 3 (January 1880).

Millard, Bailey. "State Road from a Private Purse." *Technical World Magazine* (July 1912).

"Monthly Record of Current Events." *Harper's New Monthly Magazine* 19, no. 112 (September 1859).

Osborne, Duffield. "Surf and Surf Bathing." *Scribner's Magazine* 8, no. 1 (July 1890).

"The Oyster Trade." *Living Age* 24, no. 305 (March 23, 1850).

"The Point of View." *Scribner's Magazine* 16, no. 4 (October 1894).

Rumford, Samuel Canby. "Early Automobiles." *Delaware History* 24, no. 2 (Fall/Winter 1990).

Spears, John R. "Sand Waves at Henlopen and Hatteras." *Scribner's Magazine* 8, no. 4 (October 1890).

Warren, T. Robinson. "Bay Shooting." *Scribner's Magazine* (December 1876).

WEBSITES

Hartwell, Joe. "*U-117.*" http://freepages.military.rootsweb.ancestry.com/~cacunithistories/U_117.html.

———. "USS *Minnesota BB-22.*" http://freepages.military.rootsweb.ancestry.com/~cacunithistories/USS_Minnesota.html.

Heintze, James R. "A Tradition of Celebration by the Adams Family." http://gurukul.american.edu/heintze/Adams.htm.

Kelly, James. "A Full and True Discovery of All the Robberies, Pyracies, and other Notorious Actions of that Famous English Pyrate, Capt. James Kelly, 1700." http://www.galapagos.to/TEXTS/KELLY.HTM.

Newman, Scott A. "Jazz Chicago: Urban Leisure from 1893 to 1945." http://chicago.urban-history.org/ven/pks/c_beach.shtml.

Tarow, Susan, trans. "The Written Record of the Voyage of 1524 of Giovanni da Verrazano as recorded in a letter to Francis I, King of France, July 8th, 1524." http://bc.barnard.columbia.edu/~lgordis/earlyAC/documents/verrazan.htm.

BOOKS

Annual Reports of the Operations of the United States Life-Saving Service. Washington, D.C.: Government Printing Office, 1889–1913.

Beach, Jack. *This Was Rehoboth Beach: Flotsam, Jetsam and Trivia.* Lewes, DE: Media Associates, 1993.

Brittingham, Hazel D. "The Fall of the Cape Henlopen Lighthouse." In *The Delaware Estuary: Rediscovering a Forgotten Resource.* Edited by Tracey L. Bryant and Jonathan R. Pennock. Philadelphia: The Philadelphia Press, 1988.

Carter, Dick. *Clearing New Ground: The Life of John G. Townsend Jr.* Wilmington: Delaware Heritage Press, 2001.

———. *The History of Sussex County.* Rehoboth Beach, DE: Community News Corporation, 1976.

Federal Writers' Project. *Delaware: A Guide to the First State.* Dover: Delaware Heritage Press, 2006.

Floyer, John. *The History of Cold Bathing.* London: 1725.

Frebert, George J. *Delaware Aviation History.* Dover, DE: Dover Litho Printing Co., 1998.

Gentile, Gary. *Shipwrecks of Delaware and Maryland.* Philadelphia: Gary Gentile Productions, 1990.

Hancock, Harold B. *Delaware Two Hundred Years Ago: 1780–1800.* Wilmington, DE: The Middle Atlantic Press, 1987.

Hayman, John C. *Rails Along the Chesapeake: A History of Railroading on the Delmarva Peninsula, 1827–1978.* Pittsburgh: Marvadel Publishers, 1979.

Horle, Craig W. *Records of the Courts of Sussex County, Delaware 1677–1710.* Philadelphia: University of Pennsylvania Press, 1991.

Jordan, Francis. *The Remains of an Aboriginal Encampment at Rehoboth Delaware.* Philadelphia: 1880.

Lencek, Lena, and Gideon Bosker. *The Beach, The History of Paradise on Earth.* New York: Viking, The Penguin Group, Penguin Putnam Inc., 1998.

Lendum, John. *Rise of Methodism in America.* Philadelphia: 1859.

Meehan, James D. *Rehoboth Beach Memoirs: From Saints to Sinners.* Bethany Beach, DE: Harold E. Dukes Jr., Publisher, 2000.

Mills, Eric. *Chesapeake Rumrunners of the Roaring Twenties.* Centreville, MD: Tidewater Publishers, 2000.

Morison, Samuel Eliot. *The European Discovery of America: The Northern Voyages.* New York: 1971.

Mullin, Gerald. *Flight and Rebellion: Slave Resistance in Eighteenth-Century Virginia.* New York: Oxford University Press, 1974.

Murphy, Henry C. *The Voyages of Verrazzano*. New York: 1875.

Noble, Dennis L. *That Others Might Live: The U.S. Life-Saving Service, 1878–1915*. Annapolis, MD: Naval Institute Press, 1994.

Paine, Ralph D. *The Book of Buried Treasure: Being a True History of the Gold, Jewels, and Plate of Pirates, Galleons, etc., which Are Sought For to This Day*. New York: Arno Press, 1981.

A Paradise for Gunners and Anglers. Philadelphia: Philadelphia, Wilmington and Baltimore Railroad Company, 1883.

Ritchie, Robert C. *Captain Kidd and the War against the Pirates*. New York: Barnes and Noble, 2006.

Scharf, J. Thomas. *History of Delaware, 1609–1888*. 2 vols. Philadelphia: 1888.

Seibold, David J., and Charles J. Adams. *Shipwrecks and Sea Stories & Legends of the Delaware Coast*. Barnegat Light, NJ: Exeter House Books, 1989.

Shanks, Ralph, and Wick York. *The U.S. Life-Saving Service: Heroes, Rescues and Architecture of the Early Coast Guard*. Edited by Lisa Woo Shanks. Petaluma, CA: Costano Books, 1998.

Stevenson, Jay. *Rehoboth of Yesteryear*. Vol. 2. Millsboro, DE: 1981.

Terrell, Dan. *Room for One More Sinner*. Rehoboth Beach, DE: 1984.

War Damage Corporation Policy. Rehoboth Historical Society, n.d.

Weslager, C.A. *Delaware's Buried Past: A Story of Archaeological Adventure*. New Brunswick, NJ: Rutgers University Press, 1968.

Weslager, C.A., and Louise Heite. *The Delaware Estuary: Rediscovering a Forgotten Resource*. Edited by Tracey L. Bryant and Jonathan R. Pennock. Newark: University of Delaware Sea Grant College Program, 1998.

Williams, William H. *Slavery and Freedom in Delaware, 1639–1865*. Wilmington, DE: Scholarly Resources, 1996.

Wilson, E. Emerson. *Forgotten Heroes of Delaware*. Cambridge, MA: Deltos Publishing, 1970.

Winslow, Julian D. *Sussex Awakens to the Toot*. Wilmington, DE: Julian D. Winslow, 1999.

ABOUT THE AUTHOR

Michael Morgan has been writing freelance newspaper articles on the history of Rehoboth Beach and the mid-Atlantic region for over three decades. He is the author of the "Delaware Diary," which appears weekly in the *Delaware Coast Press*, and the "Sussex Journal," which is a weekly feature of the *Wave*. Morgan has also published articles in the *Baltimore Sun, Maryland Magazine, Chesapeake Bay Magazine, Civil War Times, World War II Magazine, America's Civil War* and other national publications. A frequent lecturer in the coastal region, Morgan's look at history is marked by a lively, storytelling style that has made his writing and lectures popular. Michael Morgan is also the author of *Pirates and Patriots: Tales of the Delaware Coast*, which captures the broad panorama of the history of the coastal region.

Visit us at
www.historypress.net